You are a complete disappointment. You are a failure. You think you are a hotshot in New York writing books, but you're not. No one wants to read your shit. It's obvious you don't even like yourself. You are broken and need to be fixed. You aren't as smart as you think you are. And you are the only person in this family who is fat. I resent you because you are having more fun than I did at your age. I didn't begin to have fun until I was fifty-five. You are a complete ointment. You are a failure. You think you are a hotshot in New York writing books not. No one wants to read your shit. It's obvious you don't even like yourself. You a eed to be fixed. You aren't as smart as you think you are. And you are the only pers who is fat. I resent you because you are having more fun than I did at your age. I di ve fun until I was fifty-five. You are a complete disappointment. You are a failure. Y hotshot in New York writing books, but you're not. No one wants to read your shit. I 't even like yourself. You are broken and need to be fixed. You aren't as smart as you re the only person in this family who is fat. I resent you because you are having mor than I did at your age. I didn't begin to have fun until I was fifty-five.
You are a complete disappointment. And you are the only person in this family who is fat.

YOU ARE A
COMPLETE
DISAPPOINTMENT

YOU ARE A
COMPLETE
DISAPPOINTMENT

A Triumphant Memoir
of Failed Expectations

Mike Edison

STERLING
New York

STERLING
New York

An Imprint of Sterling Publishing, Co., Inc.
1166 Avenue of the Americas
New York, NY 10016

ISBN 978-1-4549-1868-4

Distributed in Canada by Sterling Publishing Co., Inc.
c/o Canadian Manda Group, 664 Annette Street
Toronto, Ontario, Canada M6S 2C8
Distributed in the United Kingdom by GMC Distribution Services
Castle Place, 166 High Street, Lewes, East Sussex, England BN7 1XU
Distributed in Australia by Capricorn Link (Australia) Pty. Ltd.
P.O. Box 704, Windsor, NSW 2756, Australia

For information about custom editions, special sales, and premium and
corporate purchases, please contact Sterling Special Sales at 800-805-5489 or
specialsales@sterlingpublishing.com.

Manufactured in the United States of America

2 4 6 8 10 9 7 5 3 1

www.sterlingpublishing.com

For Mom and Dad and all the wounded cats and kittens,
with love.

If you are living for tomorrow,
you will always be one day behind.

—BILL HICKS

CONTENTS

"YOU ARE A COMPLETE DISAPPOINTMENT"

My father was having a hard time speaking.

He was on his deathbed, quite literally, in an Arizona hospital room—the best money could buy, with all sorts of tubes exploding out of his arms, monitors beeping and buzzing, nurses bustling in and out to check the connections and interpret the blizzard of numbers that flashed on and off like Christmas lights on a Matterhorn of rack-mounted biotech, a pinball parlor's worth of LED readouts that could just as easily have been designed to read EXTRA BALL or SPECIAL WHEN LIT. He was breathing erratically through a milky plastic oxygen mask that was growing thick with condensation.

He waved me over to the bed.

"I'm glad you're here," he began. "There is something I want to tell you."

I sidled up close to hear what he had to say.

There was a soft sucking sound from inside the mask, and the low whistle and *shhhhhhhh* of an air valve doing its thing. His eyes were clear, lucid blue.

"You," he said, "are a complete disappointment."

He sucked another lungful of oxygen out of the mask, and his eyes opened up like saucers. He was just getting started.

"You are a failure," he leveled, gaining strength. "You think you are a hotshot in New York writing books, but you're not. No one wants to read your shit. It's obvious you don't even like yourself," he added, before turning to my younger brother, the Wall Street *macher* who was standing next to me, wearing a dirty T-shirt from a recent Who reunion concert, cargo shorts, and those trendy, Fruity Pebbles®–colored plastic clogs. "It's been a pleasure to watch *you* grow up," he said to him.

My father's breathing had become a Greek chorus of pulmonary angst, like Darth Vader, if Darth Vader were an old Jewish man who lay dying in a hospital bed. After another air-valve intermezzo—*hhoooooaaaawhhhk*—he turned his attention back to me. "You are broken," he said, "and need to be fixed."

Never mind his immediate challenges—the mask, the tubes, the electrodes, the IV drip, the demoralizing, disposable pale-green hospital gown—the old man delivered his message right over the plate.

"You aren't as smart as you think you are," he hacked. "And," he added, after taking a moment to catch his breath, an increasingly rare commodity, and marshaling every bit of strength he could, leaning forward like the carved wooden mast on a pirate ship and spitting into his oxygen mask, "you are the only person in this family who is fat."

If his vitriol were a baseball, they would have said it had some mustard on it. I was speechless, and I watched it sail by without swinging, as stoic as Kaw-Liga, the famous cigar-store Indian. There wasn't much else I could do. Not to set the bar of what it means to be a *mensch* too low, but there was no way I was going to fight with a breathless, dying man.

The truth is that my father never liked me very much. For years he railed at me, with no attempt to reserve his anger: "I resent you because you are having more fun than I did at your age. I didn't begin to have fun until I was fifty-five."

I had heard variations of this tune my whole life, recurring themes of jealousy and contempt. When I was nineteen and my band was beginning to see some moderate success, being booked for tours of Europe, he hissed: "I hate that you get to live your dreams before I get to live mine."

Twenty years later, when I began shopping my first book—a memoir largely about my dubious double-helix of a career as musician and magazine editor—he opened fire: "No one wants to read your shit. No one cares about you." When I told him I thought I had some serious interest from a legit publisher, he assured me, "It's not going to happen." When I told him, no, everything is looking good, that I was pretty sure I was going to get a good offer, he demanded, "Oh yeah? How much do you want to bet?"

I called him back a few weeks later and apologized *to him* for getting heated, never mind that he had put *his money* on *my failure.* If I didn't make that call, we could have gone forever without speaking again, and I wasn't quite ready for that. So I decided to suck it up and be "big," as they say. But here in the hospital room I was starting to discover that being "big" was totally overrated.

With every new volley, he became more and more agitated. His blood pressure was punching a hole in the sky, and his oxygen level was going south fast—you didn't need a degree in advanced medical engineering to know that the numbers racing on the readouts weren't the good news everyone had been hoping for. Then again, seething as he was, he wasn't really helping his own cause.

A fresh phalanx of nurses came crashing in like a Navy SEAL team to try to calm him. It was fucking scary, and it was fucking weird, although I am still not sure if it was John Waters weird or David Lynch weird. It certainly wasn't any fun.

And then he dropped the bomb, his last great mortal concern. This is what had turned disgust into ire, and ire into top-fuel rage. He leaned forward, fighting the trauma team so he could spit it out from behind the oxygen mask, which was now opaque with saliva and spew, and he let me have it: "I can't believe someone as smart as you likes professional wrestling!"

It was the last thing he ever said to me.

WHENEVER I TELL THE STORY, people laugh. And then they apologize for laughing, because they can't believe someone could be so mean, and they don't want to seem heartless or unfeeling, and then they laugh some more, because the irony of a poignant deathbed scene turned comically sour outweighs the bizarro-world cruelty of the whole lousy affair. It's a just lot easier to laugh than to try and parse the brutality of it all. It never fails.

"'A complete disappointment'? You mean like one of those shitty Star Wars prequels? Bwwwahhhhh!"

"'You are broken and need to be fixed'?? Oh, that's priceless."

"'You don't even like yourself'??? Oh, you have got to be kidding . . . Does he even know you? Hahahahaha . . ."

And then, because my friends are largely a kind lot, they strive to reassure me of my value in this world, but by the time I get to the bit about being too smart to like professional wrestling, what they really want to know is how something so self-consciously silly can tie a guy up in knots so fucking tight that this is what has consumed him during his last moments on Earth. Why is it even part of the conversation? And it's not like all my friends are wrestling fans—the great majority of them think it is far too dumb for even their slightest consideration, and they mostly just tolerate my enthusiasm, laughing with me occasionally but all fairly certain that I have committed worse crimes.

MY FATHER SUFFERED FROM MORE than a little bit of status anxiety, which was ridiculous, because he came from a lovely Boston home, went to the best schools, and became extremely successful in business. Nevertheless, his main concern always seemed to be how others perceived him.

I always say it takes a little bit of crazy to keep the big crazy away, but he led a life terrified of cutting loose, lest he appear out of control or, God forbid, *frivolous*. Frivolity was a big, frilly no-no. He was driven by what Paul Fussell once called "anxious gentility." He made taste decisions based largely on social aspirations, and my querulous love of the lowbrow somehow threatened to turn his world topsy-turvy.

My father reminded me of my favorite cartoon fish, Charlie® the Tuna. People of a certain age are sure to remember the old animated StarKist® Tuna television ads. They went like this: Charlie's one goal in life was to be accepted by the StarKist Tuna company. This was, for a tuna fish, the ultimate status symbol, never mind that "acceptance" in this case would mean being filleted and canned and stuffed into sandwiches and mediocre casseroles. Charlie strove to get the nod. He wore a pretentious beret and some very smart-looking eyeglasses. In one television advertisement, he was playing a harp—plucking away at one note with the aplomb of a virtuoso. His friend, an octopus jamming on flute, says to him, "Hey Charlie, you're only playing one note!" Charlie says, "It's a great note! Mozart used it lots of times! Hey, StarKist, listen to my musical good taste . . ."

But in every spot he is rebuffed: "Sorry, Charlie. Star-Kist doesn't want tunas with good taste; they want tunas that taste good!"

Class consciousness informed my father in all things, and to him there was nothing lower than wrestling fans. They were "toothless hicks and hillbillies," the absolute nadir of the human race, a pop-culture pathology that festered between the pit of his fears and the summit of his disdain. "That's not who we are," he chided me, "We are better than *that*."

I have no idea why he thought wrestling fans were from the South or were immune from the miracles of modern dentistry, and why he somehow felt entitled to pronounce judgment on everyone around him, but there you have it. He was a bit of a pill.

A few nights ago I was recounting the deathbed story to a friend of mine: "And so I go over to the bed, and I say 'Yes, Dad?' And he leans in and says, 'You are a complete disappointment.'"

"Oh, shit," my friend says, laughing cautiously. "Wow, I'm so sorry that happened to you. It reminds me of my old man. After I got out of school and had my first big job interview, he told me, 'They don't want people like you.'"

Lately I've been getting a lot of that. The more I tell the story, the more I realize that there are a lot of fathers out there who somehow along the way were stripped of their kindness and their compassion for their children. Dads who compete with their sons and drive them to acting out are legend. I remember hearing about one guy who started a war in Iraq to impress his old man.

My father harbored a galaxy's worth of unrealistic expectations and a narcissist's obsession with perfection. He had never been liberated from the truculence of seeking status through the petty tyranny of taste. Outwardly he was the very picture of affability—a popular guy, a master of small talk. But, having somehow earned a lifetime's worth of his ire, to me he was a scion of dysfunction.

By the way, I guess it's worth mentioning that the friend of mine I was just talking about graduated from Columbia University in the same class as Barack Obama.

"So what was your father so upset about?" I asked him.

"I don't think he liked my taste in music," he told me.

I PRIDE MYSELF ON MY GOOD TASTE in movies, wine, women, detective novels, eyeglasses, electric guitars, neckties, nightclubs—you name it. I recoil in horror when someone puts cheese on pastrami or, God forbid, mayonnaise on a corned beef sandwich. When I am on a first date and the woman I am with orders a "vodka and soda" without calling a brand of vodka, it is a deal-breaker.

Seriously, if you somehow made it to forty years old and are still drinking vodka from the well, it is pretty clear that the fabulous dinner we are about to have is going to be lost on you.

Cheap vodka aside, the true definition of a snob is someone who is so invested in class and status, they actually believe that how much money you make or where you went to school somehow dictates your value as a person. And that ain't me—I'm just a guy who is passionate about a lot of different stuff. You know, curiosity killed the cat, but satisfaction brought him back.

I would be disingenuous if I said I don't *ever* care about what other people think about my taste. I like to look presentable—*dashing*, even—on a date, on a gig, or if anyone ever called me again for a job interview. I have a closet full of suits and vintage deco ties, slightly starched white shirts with collars cut like razors, cowboy shirts with ornate embroidery and pearl buttons, fedoras for every season, square-toed mod boots that work for any occasion, socks with clocks on them right out of the Philip Marlowe collection, and a gorilla suit that gets a lot more play than you would ever imagine. Everyone loves a man in a gorilla suit.

Someday I would very much like to wear a black turtleneck because I think it is a good look for a middle-aged beatnik. But I don't, because I am also self-conscious enough to know that wearing a turtleneck sweater makes me look like an *actual turtle*. It sucks having a fat neck and a round head. But I never really cared what anyone thought about my fetish for old blues singers, which made me kind of an odd duck to the girls I knew in high school, and I clearly don't care what anyone thinks about my enthusiasm for men-in-tights, whether they're cater-wauling in the Ring cycle or just a smelly old ring. A little bit of benign connoisseurship never hurt anyone. At any rate, it would give us something to talk about if we ever got stuck together in an airport bar, or on a first date.

My father's brand of snobbery was particularly nasty. He pretended to be folksy and unpretentious when nothing could be farther than the truth. And he could be vicious. Just as much as he cozied up to those whom he thought might help elevate his social status, he punched down at those he deemed below him. He ridiculed my mother for being a "brand whore" because she carried a Gucci® bag. It was, to him, *ostentatious*—he considered designer clothes and accessories an overreach by people who had no class in the first place. But when it came to badging oneself with name brands, he was just as bad, except he chose marks that promoted a patina of affluent, post-preppy perfection, never really appreciating that the bespoke humility of Brooks Brothers® purred just as loudly as the bourgeois status bump of the Gucci bag.

High on the no-fly list, along with Louis Vuitton®
luggage, Liberace, and a litany of my childish pleasures
(amusement parks, horror movies, and comic books
among them), were the great American trilogy of motor-
cycles, guns, and tattoos. Which begs the question: Why
the hell did he decide to retire to Arizona, where every
other person has at least one of those things? Going to
the supermarket must have been intolerable.

Someone I know who lives in Arizona and had been
to my dad's house laughed at the scenario: "The people
like your dad who live in these gated golf-course com-
munities, they want to tie their identity with the spirit of
the Old West. And it makes them feel precious to live in
the Southwest among all of this beauty so they can brag
to their friends back east, but they want no part of the
reality of who and what actually lives and thrives here.
Where they live, all the natural fauna has been removed.
There are no thorns *anywhere*. It's kind of an ecological
crime. It's the only place in the desert where there is
Kentucky bluegrass."

In wrestling parlance, this is called "kayfabe"—
holding up the illusion that everything you see is real.
It's maintaining the gimmick at all times, meaning the
sadistic Marine Drill Sergeant you see on television
battling the Russian Heathen is actually a sadistic
Marine Drill Sergeant in real life, and the Russian is

without equivocation our biggest threat to losing the Cold War. And, after they are done working, they do not go to parent-teacher conferences or mow the lawn, and they especially do not have drinks together at the hotel bar. They are 100 percent legit enemies, the bona-fide bone-snapping Marine and the unrepentant Commie Thug.

In the old days, when a large part of the wrestling audience still thought that what they were watching was "real," it was considered taboo to "break kayfabe." Everyone stayed in character, always, to protect the business, and no one told tales out of school. No out-of-character interviews or public behavior, ever. It is what we call a "work." The opposite of this is called a "shoot"— which just means "straight-shooting." A lot of wresting slang comes from old carnival put-ons, like the gallery games that were stocked with rifles fixed so "the mark" could never hit the target and win the big prize. Straight-shooting meant the guns weren't gimmicked; they were true. Ready, aim, fire.

Losing control in the hospital room was my father's true self betraying his gimmick of genteel perfection. It was the sedition of his glands. But at least it was real—a pure *shoot*. With his last breath, this was the message he was most compelled to deliver: "You are a complete disappointment." And he threw it for a strike.

I truly wanted to like my dad, and I desperately wanted him to like me. No matter what—for our entire lives together—that never stopped. When he finished his onslaught, I left that room a heartbroken mess.

It was far too soon to see a bigger picture and try to find some compassion for him. That would come in time. For the moment, though, while he was being carted off to die, I was devastated. It had been a hell of a speech, with lots of points scored for style. And that comment about being smart and liking wrestling really rankled. It was as idiotically mundane and petulant as it was bizarre and existentially horrifying. What had happened to him that had made him so angry? I know he hated my lowbrow taste, but how did this disdain became so pathologically profound that he perceived my every small success as an insurgent uprising, and my fondness for spectacle as a personal threat. How had head-butts and spangly tights become the catalyst for a lifetime's worth of filial contempt? Maybe he had a bad wrestling experience. Maybe André the Giant stole his girl? I have no idea. At least I was not going to be wondering anymore if I would ever hear him say, *I am proud of you.* That ship had sailed. Like the *Titanic.*

Perhaps if he had allowed himself, just once, to stoop low enough to watch one of the crappy science-fiction movies I had loved so much as a kid, he would have learned that you cannot clone yourself—you cannot create a new world in your own image.

It never works.

Someone always gets hurt.

2

OF ATOMIC FIREBALLS
AND TALKING COWS

I was about seven years old the first time I tried Atomic FireBalls, the hard, super-spicy cinnamon candies that burn hot and sweet and make your mouth all red. I think I was just attracted to the packaging—there was a mushroom cloud on the box that spoke to their genuine atomic power—and decided to give them a go, rather than buy my usual ZotZ®.

ZotZ, if you recall, were hard candies filled with a sour, fizzy powder. Bicarbonate of crap, I think it was called, and when you got to the center (meaning when you broke it in half with one good crunch), your entire mouth was filled with foamy white stuff, which (if you had some good technique) you could make trickle out over your lips as if you were having a seizure. It was kind of gross and kind of cool, and when we were just a little bit older we definitely realized that it had some odd sexual overtones, like the bubble gum filled with liquid that squirted into your mouth when you bit down on it.

Atomic FireBalls were nothing short of a gut punch—the first "hot" food that I had ever tried—and they thrust the rest of my flavorless suburban life into the shadows. Everything else sucked. Atomic FireBalls ruled. They would be my new religion.

"You've got to try one of these!" I insisted to my dad, evangelical in my exuberance that this was the single greatest thing that had ever happened to me. "They're fantastic!"

"No, I am not going to try one of those, whatever they are," he told me, showing his disapproval with what I would come to know as a well-practiced look of utter disgust. Then he made a big show of offering me his candy of choice, Necco® wafers, which were quarter-sized disks that tasted like old waxed paper and grout that I pretended to like because I wanted to have something I could share with my father. I didn't want to hurt his feelings by spitting the foul thing out on the floor, which was my first instinct, and I later found out that tasting as if they had been left on the shelf since the Civil War was actually their biggest selling point—it took a special kind of rank, gastronomic nostalgia to eat them.

The Atomic FireBall was ground zero for the Taste Wars, and from there a lifetime's worth of absurd Father

v. Son ad hominem challenges began. Pretty much right up until he died, every time I tried something new and liked it, whether it was a breakfast cereal or a new pizza topping—if I had the audacity to try and share it—I was rebuffed and told to "grow up."

It's ridiculous, I know, but when I was a child, I was constantly told to "just grow up already." Seven years old and already I was being indicted for the crime of "immaturity," which Ambrose Bierce might have described as "the word old people use to put down younger people who have more fun than they do," never mind the absurdity of measuring a second grader's choices in candy, cartoons, and breakfast cereal against that of an Ivy-educated suburban father of three, or the insanity of pushing his Eisenhower-era tastes onto the palate of a kid who had just entered the Brave New World of Atomic FireBalls—which, I can tell you now, was most definitely a gateway to harder stuff (Tabasco® sauce, jalapeños, tequila, LSD, etc).

Later, I came to realize that my dad's childhood had been deflated by similarly unimaginative parents. He was born of adults who somehow skipped or just repressed the ecstasy and horrors and general confusion of being young, adults who were incapable of experiencing the travails—joyful, playful, sad, hurt, whatever—of their own children. His folks were society stiffs who would never get down on the floor and crawl around on the carpet with their toddlers. They weren't huggers or listeners, and they certainly didn't know how to be silly, or play games, or have any sort of fun that strayed from their uptight parochial formulary, and it stuck with him when he had kids of his own.

Throughout my childhood he made fun of me all the time for what I watched on television: popular sitcoms like *Happy Days* and *Good Times*, which the kids in school liked to talk about at lunchtime, seeing who could do the best imitations of the Fonz or Jimmy "Dyn-O-Mite" Walker; *Chiller Theatre*, which showed mostly B horror films like *The Brain That Wouldn't Die*, *Attack of the Crab Monsters*, and *Psychomania* (a British biker-horror masterpiece about a motorcycle gang that came back from the dead—they were actually buried on their choppers and rode them straight out of the grave, which is every bit as awesome as it sounds); *Creature Features*, which favored old-school Universal Studios monster movies (*The Mummy* was my favorite) and Christopher Lee's slightly risqué Dracula flicks; and, of course, *Championship Wrestling*, which came on at ten o'clock on Saturday mornings, followed by the roller derby that I loved but could not for the life of me ever figure out how they kept score.

He took special glee in mocking me for watching the wrestling—*It's fake! It's not real! Grow up! How dumb can you be?* But truthfully, even at seven years old, I knew in my heart of hearts it wasn't legit. How could it be? We all had heard the rumors that Chief Jay Strongbow was really an Italian guy from the Bronx, and even a blind man could see the pulled punches from a mile away. But then, like now, it didn't matter. It was a world unconfined by the laws and rules the rest of us had to obey. In wrestling there was *justice*, and there was *freedom*. Wrestling was all about the power of *imagination*.

Then, and as ever, I championed the bad guys, and especially their preposterous manager-cum-mouthpieces, for whom it was a Golden Era, led by a triumvirate of lunatics: "Captain Lou" Albano, who spat when he talked and inexplicably had rubber bands attached to his face, like some sort of escaped mental patient; the Grand Wizard of Wrestling, a shriveled Jewish man who wore hideous madras jackets, sparkly turbans, and wrap-around shades and who claimed to be the smartest man in the world; and "Classy" Freddie Blassie, the self-proclaimed "King of Men" who even had his own hilarious song, "Pencil Neck Geeks." They were larger than life. They oozed a certain retarded charisma that I still find irresistible.

Anyway, when my dad told me to "grow up" at age seven, I knew even then it was ridiculous. I probably rolled my eyes and went back to watching *Kung Fu Theater* and stuffing my mouth with ZotZ just to see how much foam

I could spew. Even then I was never really one for "growing up," such as it was. I was always more about *evolving*.

ONCE THE WAR STARTED, it never relented. Penny candy was just the beginning. I remember vividly when I was ten years old and wanted to play Little League® baseball, and he told me, "No, you don't. You're not good at it. Do you really want to embarrass yourself?" While I probably wasn't ever going to be the league's all-star first baseman, I could certainly hit and run and catch enough not to embarrass myself, or him—which I now know was all he really cared about. My lack of perfection at the plate was more a liability to his perception of himself as a flawless human than it could ever be to a bunch of little kids, none of whom were future Hall of Famers.

The fucked-up thing is that he was so deadly convincing in his scouting report that I actually believed him, and for a long time I had zero confidence whenever I played baseball or stickball—or even kickball, the most dumbed-down, skill-less variant of the lot. It took most of my adolescence to realize that I actually was coordinated enough to kick a big rubber ball across a playground, never mind smack the shit out of a baseball. Of course what I realize now is that this was just his way of saying,

"Anything that involves wearing a T-shirt with the name of a pizzeria on the back can't possibly be worthwhile." Little League was vulgar in the truest sense.

He was in perfect form when my first attempt at playing music netted me an alto saxophone in the fourth grade. From the very first day I brought that baby home and polished it up and put it on in front of the mirror to see how cool it looked, the old man told me to give it up. "You're no good at it," he barked. "You're not musical."

At first it probably sounded like outtakes from an Ornette Coleman record. That's what happens when you stick a saxophone in a ten-year-old's mouth. It might have even been pretty good in its primitive, harmolodic innocence, but there was no way my father was ever going to be ready for that. A year later, when I had figured out how to play the first few bars to the solo on "Brown Sugar" and a little bit of "Whatever Gets You Through the Night" and was starting to get a firm handle on this whole saxophone thing, he was still ridiculing me, really making sure I got the message: *You suck!*

After he was obligated to come hear me play in the school band at one of those springtime assemblies that are supposed to promote confidence in the kids, he let me know in no uncertain terms just how awful it was. On the spot he canceled our post-concert date to go to Carvel® for ice cream with all the other kids ("You don't deserve it"), and told me again that it would be best if I gave it all up. The next day at school, I had to explain to everyone why I wasn't at the ice cream parlor. My career as a sax player died soon after, even as my teacher encouraged me to stay at it.

When I was eleven and had my next bright idea—to play the drums—he didn't miss a beat. At first I thought he had come around to rewarding my enthusiasm by buying me the secondhand drum set I had found by scouring the local classifieds. I had begged for the set vociferously (it cost fifty bucks—which I was expected to pay back in full), but it turned out to have more pieces missing than were actually there, and this time he yelled at me because I didn't play it right away.

"But Dad, there's no bass drum pedal, no cymbals, and no seat! Also I need some sticks!"

"Good musicians don't blame their instruments. You should probably quit now. Obviously you aren't mature enough. You need to grow up."

My true dream when I was in sixth grade, however, was to work for *MAD Magazine*. I even sent them my own contributions: largely primitive interpretations of Don Martin's crazy sound effects (*Spwatch! Spwizzle! Glbble! Sprack! Foinsapp!*) and the characters he drew, with their outsized chins and folded-over feet. Not surprisingly, I never heard back from them.

Actually I wasn't bad for a little kid. Every year I would have something that I drew chosen to represent my elementary school in some art fair and competition, and they'd put it up at the local shopping mall. One year I even won a blue ribbon—first prize! Surely I was going places! Maybe I could even have a strip in the newspaper, like the guy who did *Peanuts,* or *Funky Winkerbean,* which wasn't even that good. I thought about it all the time.

My mother always encouraged me, but she saw any artistic proclivity I may have had as not much more than a charming hobby. The very second I started making noise about actually becoming an artist, she stopped thinking it was so cute. And the only kudos I got from my father for being good with a pen or brush were when he demanded I make greeting cards for him whenever he needed one, in which case I would whip one up—usually a cow saying "Happy Birthday," or whatever the occasion was. For some reason I thought drawing talking cows was hilarious, and this a good four years before I started smoking pot. I guess, no matter what age you are, there is something existentially subversive about a talking cow.

I was always happy to whip up all manners of cards and greetings because I thought he was proud of me and wanted to show off my skills. Later I realized he just didn't like to buy store-bought cards (he considered them not only a waste of money, but also the same sort of déclassé crap embraced by the peons who participated in things like Little League and bake sales). He had less-than-zero interest in my earnest attempts at breaking into *MAD Magazine* ("They don't want you, stop wasting your time"). I started feeling more like a trained monkey than an admired or loved child, and I stopped doing tricks on demand. Somehow he had turned my chorus of bovine hilarity into a big mess of rotten burger meat, and I no longer wanted any part of it.

IRONICALLY, IT WAS LARGELY THANKS to my dad that I got into photography, which eventually led me to the bright idea of going to film school—an experience I think we would both rate as a failure, although for different reasons. His own pictures were gorgeous. I am looking at one now: a beautiful black-and-white matte print of us in the park on an autumn day. The leaves are slightly out of focus, a deft use of depth of field, and us kids pop out in front of them, crisp and clear. The composition is rock-solid, the lighting, beyond criticism. My brothers, nine years old at the time, are wearing white cable-knit sweaters and have big smiles, while I—on the cusp of my turn as a teenage beatnik—am wearing a dark sweater and a coy half grin. It's my favorite photograph of us, but in no way does it reflect the nightmare it was to actually have it taken.

Those days in the park taking pictures were torture for everyone involved, but especially for my mom, who hated to see us being yelled at to stand or sit silently. My dad turned a family day in the park into an anal compulsive's campaign to have perfect pictures of his perfect kids, shot in a style that demonstrated his own perfect taste and mastery of the photographic art. There was much yelling and, sometimes, crying. Great photos, though.

He would send the negatives to a lab in New York City and get them back with contact sheets, which he would pore over with a plastic loupe and mark with a grease pencil, which I was never allowed to touch. These were *tools*, not *toys*, and first I would have to learn to take pictures—and then, *maybe* then, if I were ever *mature* enough, I would be allowed entry into the palace where one looked at contact sheets and made what seemed like cataclysmic decisions about what to have printed, and always in matte finish, he explained, because that showed he had good taste. Also, it cost more than the glossy finish. That was somehow important, too.

At first he was excited when I bought a used single-lens reflex camera with paper-route money and listened ardently to his advice about f-stops and shutter speeds. I took a few shots of my younger brothers that met with his approval, and I aspired to have a Nikon® F camera, just like his. I was so happy that I had discovered something he liked and that I was actually good at. I was trying so hard to please him. Then something happened: I won a photo contest in the local paper, and suddenly the Nikon I had been saving up for, the one just like his, was "too much camera" for me. I didn't need it. Also, I was warned, photography was a "very expensive hobby," so maybe I ought to think about that a little, too, and maybe I should stop now. If he knew all of this was going to lead to film school, he probably would have carved out my eyes with his grease pencil.

But an aunt thoughtfully gave me a lovely set of Time Life® books about photography, which I studied ardently and wanted to share with my dad. There was so much information about light and composition—why, you could do anything with a camera! It beat drawing pictures of cows hands-down. It was all so exciting. Look at this guy, Robert Frank—he drove around the country taking pictures, and now he's famous! All I wanted to do was pore through this trove of knowledge and art with my dad, because, after all, he was the guy who got me into it in the first place. But it made him insane when I started playing with the camera's settings to purposely blur photos or experiment with light or composition in any way at all. He was very clear: There is a right way, and a wrong way. He thought studio photography was fake. He was an enemy of the avant-garde. My next idea, to become a photojournalist, was shot down because very few people made it. I had seen a lot of war photos in *Life*, and dreamed about being on the front lines, being the one guy who could bring back that story. I read *Rolling Stone* and *Creem* and *Circus*, and I especially liked some pictures taken of Led Zeppelin on their tour plane. That seemed like a pretty good job to have, traveling with Led Zeppelin—at least as good as going to Vietnam. But I was told, "That isn't really photography." I am sure he didn't think it was "really music," either.

Years later, someone suggested that he was just being a parent and trying to steer me toward more "realistic" career choices, but over the years I've come to understand that he was terrified of big dreams—especially anything that seemed capricious or difficult to control. Dreaming created instability. Eventually he stopped taking pictures altogether and sold me his Nikon at what he assured me was a fair price. Now I know that price-gouging me was another attempt at teaching me a lesson, that it was all out of my league, and that I needed to knock off all these silly ideas about being an artist or having any sort of glamorous career. But I was young then, and all I saw were possibilities.

3

THE GREAT MEATBALL PIZZA INCIDENT

In 1975, when I was eleven, pizza occupied a central role in my existence. Back then we had Nino's, which was favored by some of the kids because it was only forty cents a slice, right next to my elementary school on Amboy Avenue. Ferraro's up the street was fifty, and Tony's had the chutzpah to charge seventy-five.

Nino's place was always dirty, with grease-stained signs drawn in shitty marker, advertising the two-slice-and-small-soda special and the price of garlic knots, and not even taped to the wall properly. Tony's had a professional sign with clean plastic letters, and he knew how to twirl a pizza in the air, like some sort of pizza daredevil, and as you know by now, I am nothing if not a slave to the spectacle. Tony's also used better cheese and had a nice thick red sauce. Ferraro's was skimpy with the mozzarella and their sauce was thin. Any eleven-year-old could tell the difference, but considering the amount of pizza I ate, I thought I could stake my claim as a connoisseur: Nino's sucked; Ferraro's was obviously cutting corners, but passable if you only had fifty cents; and Tony's was like the Evel Knievel of pizzas.

The White Birch Inn, however, was the final frontier. It reeked of illicit sex and low-level crime—part of the extended demimonde of Routes 1 and 9, which ran together from Woodbridge up past the Rahway prison, through Linden, Elizabeth, and Newark, all the way to New York City. As far as I can remember, it was always a real piece of shit, pockmarked with as many axle-jarring incongruities as hot-sheet motels and failing businesses.

As a little kid, the motels particularly fascinated me, what with their signs for water beds, in-room movies, and mirrored ceilings, with rates by the hour, night, or week. Some of them even had pools! And as far as I could tell, there were always vacancies. One day, I reckoned, maybe I'd get a room for a few hours and go swimming and watch some of the in-room movies on one of those water beds. It seemed like it would be a lot of fun.

The White Birch was a low, white stucco building with a black roof—a real bunker of a cocktail lounge—and whenever we drove by it I was always equally fascinated and creeped out because I didn't understand why anyone would go into such a dingy-looking place, especially in the middle of the day, when adults were supposed to be working. And yet the parking lot was always full. Clearly something was happening in there, and I could not wait until I was old enough to find out exactly what. So imagine my surprise when it was announced that we would be dining there, joining our Jewish neighbors, the Goldsteins, who swore by the White Birch's thin-crust pizza.

This was just about the most exciting news I had ever heard. First, one had to drive more than five minutes to get there (which seemed ridiculous because, in my experience, no one had ever gone out of their way for pizza). Second, up until then the only other real restaurant I had ever been in with my parents was the Jade Pagoda, a dimly lit Chinese restaurant with a dusty tiki décor. My parents would order lobster Cantonese, which was exotic without being threatening, and a cheap source of lobster. Never mind that it was covered in a white sauce flecked with green scallions and looked like something Linda Blair spat up in *The Exorcist*, back in the 1970s, suburban Jews loved that shit.

The White Birch, however, was *goyish*. It was blue-collar and boozy. Up in front there was a bar lost in a gauzy haze of cigarette smoke, where guys with big collars and gold chains bought whiskey sours for the Big-Haired Ladies, with their eyes coyly darting from man to

31

man beneath curtains of blue eye shadow. My parents had no business being there. They were strangers in a strange land. Cocktails were like kryptonite to sheltered Jews who lived in fear of gentile culture (to paraphrase Lenny Bruce: *Wine* is Jewish, *cocktails* are *goyish*), and it all helped create the ticklish sense of unease that was the catalyst for what is now generally referred to as "The Great Meatball Pizza Incident."

THE GOLDSTEINS, who lived down the street, were always friendly and fairly innocuous. They had two kids—one my age, who had kind of a square head, and another a few years younger who was chubby and had some sort of speech impediment. I have no idea how they first found themselves in the White Birch—I am guessing they had some progressive-leaning gentile friends who let them in on the secret—but apparently they had experienced the same epiphany that I was now having on my first visit: This was the best pizza, ever. Suddenly it was clear as day that Tony, Nino, and the Ferraro brothers weren't much more than confidence men selling tired pie to naive children and provincial adults who had no idea of how good pizza could really be.

The White Birch pie was clearly playing in a different league. Somehow they had fallen upon the perfect sauce-to-cheese ratio—less of both than either Tony or Nino used, but more than the cheapskates at Ferraro's—and the result was to those greasy slabs what the ballet was to Black Sabbath: *elevated.* The crust was crispy and so light that it probably couldn't have sustained too much more sauce and cheese than what the geniuses at the White Birch had proportioned, anyway. This was the first time I had realized that the crust wasn't just a delivery system for toppings—it was actually maybe even the most important part of the trip—and that revelation in and of itself made me look at the world differently. It was like the first time you looked in a microscope in grade school and saw things on a cellular level, or read *Horton Hears a Who!* and got the idea that things weren't always what they seemed, that below the surface there was a lot more going on than what met the eye. I thought I could eat one hundred slices. Everyone, it seemed, agreed, and at first there was much happy munching.

Initially we ordered one large pie for us, and the Goldsteins ordered their own. We each had our own proprietary pitcher of root beer.

One of the many things my parents never really understood was family-style eating. Even at the Chinese place, apart from the pupu platter (which they ordered for two, even though we were five, and there was always a row over who was going to get the sparerib and who was going to get stuck with the shrimp toast, whatever that was), everyone ordered their own entrées, which I suspect was mostly to keep the kids away from their precious lobster Cantonese, which we weren't allowed to order because it was deemed too expensive for children to eat.

Our dinners at home weren't exactly celebrations, either. My mother clearly did not relish cooking for the family—generally the hallmark of a proud Jewish mom. The whole thing was just a major pain in the ass that involved a lot of yelling, and she never strayed too far from a horrendous rotation that was anchored in Shake 'n Bake® chicken, frozen Empire® kosher turkey breast, "Chinese" chicken baked on a cookie sheet flooded with a jar of sweet-and-sour sauce and finished with an entire can of water chestnuts, and spaghetti and meatballs drowned with extra "Old World"-style sauce. Once a week, like clockwork, we ate rare London broil, which my father carpeted with salt and inhaled like a jet engine, only chewing sporadically and making sounds similar to what you would imagine a giant, meat-eating dinosaur made while eating a smaller, inferior dinosaur. Occasionally, if she forgot to shop and we had already sent out for pizza once that week, she would make pancakes out of the mix that sat on the pantry shelf like that picture of Dorian Gray, which is why I still hate breakfast for dinner and never eat eggs after brunch.

Eventually, when my dad moved out, Mom pretty much gave up on cooking altogether, leaving us stacks of frozen pizzas, which was even worse than the stuff Nino was peddling. Fortunately, my friends took mercy on me, and I had family dinner with them and their parents a couple of times a week, which was a real eye-opener. They laughed. The parents listened to their children. They kidded one another. They talked about their days. It was as if they actually knew one another and were interested in one another's lives. Sometimes they even liked the same music! It was usually the Beatles, but nonetheless, the entire concept was astonishing. Not once in my lifetime did I ever see my parents enjoy each other or their kids. No one ever asked me what I was reading, or if I had a girlfriend, or what we were learning in American History. Dinner was the sound of my father's sloppy chewing, and the kids' squabbling, and Mom begging through her teeth for everyone to please be nice.

I don't remember what we ordered on our pizza that night at the White Birch—probably nothing, given the anemic, utterly joyless gastronomic proclivities of my parents—but the Goldsteins ordered something that my overcooked brain had not even imagined possible: a *meatball* pizza.

What was this wondrous fusion of all that was holy? Were there entire meatballs on the pizza? What kept them from rolling off? How did it work? The mind boggled. I had to know.

And the Goldsteins were only too happy to share. In fact, they were delighted to initiate me into this brave new world where meatballs and pizzas lived in peace and harmony (it turned out that the meatballs were sliced and then laid on the pizza like pepperoni). But my father was having no part of it. Mrs. Goldstein, who shared her oldest son's square-shaped head, passed me a slice of this miracle, but my dad brought his hand down to stop her. "NO," he said, "Don't eat that. We have our own."

"It's fine," said Mrs. Goldstein, who was soft-spoken and very sweet. "We have plenty, and we can always order another. You should try the meatball pie—it's delicious."

"NO! We don't eat other people's food," he barked at me. "That's *their* pizza." He was like some great, pissed-off god hurling thunderbolts down from Mount Olympus to terrorize the pizza-munching mortals, and the table froze. I suppose even the gods can be petty when they feel like it.

Elton John was playing on the jukebox: "Bennie and the Jets"—still my very favorite of his hits. Details like that tend to be painted vividly when cast against the spectacle of a man screaming about a meatball pizza, and with such fury that my little brothers either are now on the verge of tears or have already begun to cry, and the younger, speech-impaired Goldstein is bleating something horrible.

There was more yelling, my mother begging him to chill the fuck out: "It's only a piece of pizza!" My father was fighting her all the way, screaming, "We don't eat other people's food! We can afford our own!"

It was what you'd call a scene, and the worst fight I ever saw my parents get into in public. At home there was much worse, but this was just mortifying. The whole restaurant, including the Big-Haired Ladies and their pride of suitors at the bar, were all staring at us, and I'm sitting there, arm still outstretched to accept this piece of pizza, caught in the middle of the storm.

I didn't know what to do. The pizza was now in my hand, and the old man was screaming at me to give it back, and the Goldsteins were saying just take it. Mr. Goldstein, whose head was quite round in contrast with his wife and child's, was encouraging calm. And what was I supposed to do: give back a piece of pizza after it was already in my hand? That seemed like the worse option, and not because I was rebelling or showing any adolescent impudence; I was just really embarrassed at the idea of passing a piece of meatball pie back and forth in some existential tug-of-war while the old man stood over us yelling. So I pulled my arm back reluctantly, and the slice of meatball pizza dropped into my plate.

I guess at some point the yelling stopped, but by then I had been meditating on the slice of meatball pizza that had found its home in front of me and was no longer able to resist temptation. I let caution to the wind and took a bite, and let me tell you, it was all that I had ever imagined pizza could be.

We've already discussed the cheese-to-sauce ratio and the subtlety of the infrastructure (namely the crust), but those fine, spicy meatball slices suggested that you could put anything on a pizza, and in the years to come I would try, inventing over fourteen thousand variations of the stoner-approved pizza bagel, all prepared in a toaster oven.

At that moment I had no idea what precipitated the old man's meltdown, but now I know that in the *macro*, he was losing control over my mother, who had become increasingly fed up with his bullying and his parsimony and otherwise pathological relationship with money. I'm certain that this no-pizza-sharing policy was driven by some pitiful, primal fear that he'd get stuck for an extra seventy-five cents for a cup of root beer quaffed by a Goldstein, or his part of the tip would be calculated inequitably because it did not reflect the exact inventory of pizza toppings eaten by his own spawn (not to mention his crappy table manners, which, given his uptight Boston upbringing, remained something of a mystery). And in the *micro*, this just wasn't *his* kind of place: The people here were tacky, and worse, they had a fair shot at getting laid that night (I am sure that by now my mother was only sleeping in the same bed with him as a matter of convenience), and thus were winning at life despite what he must have perceived as their lousy New Jersey, Routes 1 and 9, cocktail-lounge pedigree. Besides everything else, he was still a snob, and judging the regulars at the White Birch Inn fueled his sense of superiority. All that, plus he obviously resented being shown up by a meatball pizza. That had to sting.

Years later, after my parents were separated and at war over a divorce settlement—he really dragged Mom through the mud, making her appraise twenty-year-old wedding gifts so he could write them off against any alimony or child support he would eventually have to pay, even as he was making more and more money—he suggested that he take me and my brothers out to the White Birch to get some meatball pie. There was no mention of the incident, and I thought, *Whoa, this was like the suburban Lexington and Concord—ground zero where a childhood that should have been like an episode of* The Wonder Years *turned into a bloody battlefield that left two families deeply scarred. Are you out of your mind, or just completely fucking tone-deaf?*

There was one other thing that I learned when I put that first slice of meatball pie in my maw and masticated—something that would help me across the years, even more than the endless riffs on the pizza bagel: Life could be great, if you just let it be that. Pizza and root beer and "Bennie and the Jets"—how could you possibly improve on that? Simple pleasures ruled! Happiness may or may not be fleeting, but no matter, because there was a lot of it out there to grab on to, and if you were good you could hold on to it and share it with the people you loved, and all the money in the world couldn't buy you better pizza or better root beer or better Elton John on the jukebox. This morsel of wisdom, as you can imagine, came in pretty handy years later.

DID YOU EVER HEAR SOMEONE SAY that the weirdest shit always happens when you are stoned? Well, let me ask you this: Do you really think the world is a different place and that new things happen just because *you* got high? That seems like a fairly self-centered worldview. The point is, all you have to do is open up and let the universe happen to you. Tuning in is a lot more important than turning on. When I got that sorted, locks came flying off doors.

I've come to believe that my parents were never truly happy because, simply, they never made happiness a goal. They had so many expectations that were never met that they became top-loaded with misery. They were angry all the time. They never learned how to let go and live in the moment. There they were with a table full of meatball pizza and root beer and three happy children, and they couldn't even see it for the blessing it was. This was the first time that I realized their marriage was doomed.

Listening to my folks yell and scream and stress and freak and fret and worry seemingly every second of their lives, it's no wonder I was sent fleeing in the opposite direction. They watched every dime like carrion birds; I spent money like a sailor on leave. They lived in fear of carbohydrates, fear of cholesterol, fear of sugar, fear of salt, fear of fat, fear of liquor, fear of strippers jumping out of birthday cakes. They were suspicious of Mexican food and, most likely, Mexicans. Their lives were planned to the calorie. If eating was a chore, then what else? I have empirical proof that they had sex together at least twice, but beyond that I refuse to speculate.

I know people who react with anger to every little hiccup in their day. Chinese food arrives cold, and holy shit! It's a total fucking catastrophe. Me, I'm just amazed that I can pick up the phone or push a few buttons and someone brings me an order of dumplings and some ribs. What, all of a sudden I'm the sultan of Brunei? What kind of marvelous world do we live in? If it comes cold, I just heat it up, and the next time I call someone else.

Of course in every life there are going to be broken hearts, and deaths, and illness, and bumps and bruises, and every color of existential angst and depression. Relationships are hard. Life punches back. But that still doesn't mean you get to be a prick.

Every fall, at Yom Kippur, I atone for the sin of picking on someone who was maybe just not as quick as I was when I was about eleven years old. It was just once, and I knew it was wrong, but I took advantage of my sharp tongue and I hurt someone's feelings. That was a long time ago, and to my knowledge caused no lasting harm, nor is even remembered by anyone besides me. I discussed this with a rabbi friend of mine, and he thought I was being ridiculous, that I really needed to forgive myself and move on.

He was right, of course. And if there is going to be any forgiveness in this story, I should probably start with myself. Warm me up for when I get around to the old man.

I've learned from my mistakes, which is really all it takes to forgive oneself for them. I am a much happier person than I used to be, and if there is one thing I am sure of, it is that kindness and compassion trump cruelty every time. Still, I hate the idea that there was ever a part of me that could be mean.

4

WELCOME TO THE SUMMER OF SUCK

L ater it became known as "the Summer of Suck," the time that began with the old man dying after dressing me down through an oxygen mask, quickly followed by my artist-turned-lawyer girlfriend dumping me, my employer of six years—a major publisher of music books, where I served as a senior editor—letting me go unceremoniously, even as they asked me to stay on as a freelancer and continue to edit books (basically they wanted me to keep doing my job, but in a rough economy they had lost interest in paying me a regular salary and covering my health insurance), and my Hercules of a cat finally kicking the bucket after eighteen years of sleeping next to my head.

My girlfriend was all curves and brains—she could have walked off the set of a Russ Meyer movie, but she was also a serious enough egghead. I thought I was being mature by not overthinking our relationship, but what I was actually doing was willfully ignoring the baggage she was carrying from her last failed romance because (A) the sex was great, and (B) she was a charming dinner companion, and I figured that sex and dinner had to be 70 percent of the equation, with the other 30 percent being entirely negotiable. As I like to say, what you lose on the swings, you make up on the merry-go-round.

But I had somehow missed the pitch, even as we had achieved the most intimate level of communication: meaningfully ignoring each other. Which is no joke. You can make love to a hundred people and never achieve the profound intimacy of a Sunday morning's easy silence in bed or at the breakfast table, only perforated by the occasional "What's six letters for 'Yankees iron man'?" She also brought me cans of cold beer in the shower— a nicety that cannot be overstated. But anything that broke the uncommitted relationship cycle of Eat, Drink, Fuck, Sleep, Repeat—aside from the occasional concert or movie date—was going to be a wrench in the works, and when I invited her to come with me to Chicago for a weekend to attend my nephew's bar mitzvah, it was exactly the wrong play.

She may have made the right decision to skip the bar mitzvah. It was a grotesque, nearly apocalyptic exhibition of twenty-first-century selfie culture, conspicuous consumption, and vacuity—more like a pep rally for a third-world dictator, what with the thundering sound system, massive video screens, and adoring followers being led to the dance floor by hired "motivators," than the celebration of a teenager's coming of age in the eyes of God and all that. It all left me feeling quite alone among my family, whose value system and worldview had long ago eclipsed my own.

Relative to the stadium-sized show in Chicago, my own bar mitzvah, in the summer of 1977, was like a DIY punk rock gig. The party was in the synagogue basement, and the band, which played mostly the Top 40 of the day, was led by my algebra teacher, Mr. Stein. Stevie Wonder's "Sir Duke" was my favorite radio hit that summer, and all the kids who came got a copy of the 45-rpm record to take home.

Mr. Stein was known primarily for his loud, multi-colored polyester shirts that looked as if they were spun from pastel-colored puke and for the long scar running down his face. The scar—a souvenir he got teaching math in Newark one year—actually made him look pretty tough. A kid had cut him pretty badly, and the highlight of his algebra class was always when he told the story. Even wearing one of the crazy Hawaiian shirts he favored for his music gigs, he added little cachet to an affair largely decorated with crepe paper.

But behind the cheap décor, I like to think there was at least a small dose of life lessons. Along with those tricks one needed to get through the ceremony without fucking up the *haftarah*, our rabbi—who drove to the synagogue on a Harley-Davidson®, no less—was intent on teaching moral values and the concept of selfless *tzedakah*, which is usually translated as "charity" but really means "righteousness, justness, and fairness," and stresses the moral imperative to help those less fortunate than we are. I remember at one after-school class, the topic was human suffering and what sort of inhumanity humans were capable of. (It was a fairly Christian message, too, now that I think about it.) This was right around the time Gary Gilmore was executed by a firing squad in Utah. Gilmore was a an unrepentant murderer who had demanded that the state execute him instead of keeping him on death row, and it was the center of a huge national debate. Gilmore had also insisted on a firing squad, which only threw more gas on an old-school tabloid pyre of sensationalism, murder, and justice on a biblical scale. Apparently, as the rabbi told us from the newspaper report, Gilmore lived for a full five minutes after taking five .30-30 caliber Silvertip® bullets in the chest from a fusillade of rifles fired by members of local law enforcement who had lined up to volunteer for the job. Did that seem like a long time? "Let's see," he proposed. And then he told us all to shut up for five minutes and think about it.

After what seemed like an eternity to a roomful of adenoidal bar mitzvah candidates squirming like earthworms in a bucket, he said, "Okay." There was an audible relief in the room.

"That was thirty seconds," he said. "Now go home and think about that."

And I did. That exercise made a huge impression on me, though at twelve years old I couldn't necessarily parse all the lessons he was teaching about cruelty and capital punishment, about revenge motives and justice. I went home to tell my father what the rabbi had taught us that day and got the usual brush-off. "Only tell me pleasant things," he said.

Part of being a bar (or bat) mitzvah is making a speech, and you are encouraged to be original and to speak from the heart about something important to you. Or at least that was the old model. I spoke about what we used to call "ecology," the strain of tree-hugging that used to be represented by a green flag with the Age of Aquarius–era θ symbol in the corner. I wish someone would tell me exactly when clean water became a liberal value, but in 1976 "ecology" was just a mellow hymnal for moderate hippies, the high sign that you were on board with Woodsy, the cartoon owl in those old public service ads: "Give a hoot, don't pollute."

It may have been a bit earnest or preachy coming from a thirteen-year-old, but it was sincere enough, and I am still proud of that speech. I could have ditched the politics and simply thanked my parents and the Academy and made for the receiving line like a mafia bride to collect envelopes and praise, but that's not who I am. Ironically, one thing that my father never recognized or appreciated was that, even as a kid, I had pretty high expectations for myself. We had that in common.

It had been drilled into me by our biker rabbi that a bar mitzvah was not a *graduation*; it was an *initiation*. It wasn't the *end* of something, it was a *beginning*—the celebration of the next phase of life. Of course that message has been largely lost on generations of kids raised by parents so reformed in their Judaism that they can hardly spell it, and the whole shebang has become largely a cash grab—a confirmation party of sorts for Jewish teenagers who feel no obligation to think past themselves, thrown to excess by their parents whose prime directive is to spoil the littler *pishers* and keep up with the Moscowitzes and Weinsteins who live down the street. I confess to being a little bit intimidated by all the money being spent on my nephew's hoo-haw, and I asked my brother why he thought a thirteen-year-old needed a twenty-thousand-dollar party. I was told, "Because he did something he didn't really want to do. That speech was very hard for him."

But back to the girlfriend. "C'mon," I offered, "Chicago is our kind of place. We'll go to the Art Institute. Maybe the symphony is in town. I'll take you out for a steak. We'll have hotel sex."

"ARE YOU CRAZY? I CAN'T MEET YOUR FAMILY!"

Personally, the whole idea of meeting the family ceased to be a panic-strewn event a long time ago, and at least 50 percent less so since my dad died. We were fully formed adults—forty-plus years old—and really, who gave a fuck? Families are nuts, and there isn't a goddam thing you can do about it. Anyway, they really weren't so bad—if you weren't related to them.

But I had crossed some sort of line with her—the one over which her deep anxiety and fear of commitment lurked like zombies in a cornfield—and she pretty much dumped me on the spot. She told me she preferred to "pull the bandage off," and after two years of a joyous and celebratory romance we never spoke again.

* * *

DO YOU KNOW THE MOVIE *2001: A Space Odyssey*? The
picture begins millions of years ago in the African desert,
and about half an hour in there is what has to be the most
famous jump cut in the history of cinema (*Breathless* not-
withstanding), when an ape throws a bleached femur bone
skyward, and the bone turns into a spaceship on its way
to the moon. That was me dropping out of college for the
first time. Like I said, I have always been about *evolving*.

Almost immediately after leaving New York University, I scored my first magazine gigs—admittedly a sordid
beat of sex, drugs, and professional wrestling, with occasional forays into music and politics—but I was getting
published, and I was getting paid. And then there was
the job I had writing porn novels. This was in the days
before affordable video technology, when paperback
books were still the favored delivery system for the high-
minded perv. I wound up writing twenty-eight of them
before I burned out.

I get it—dropping out of college and writing smut
was not what my parents had in mind for me. It's not
what *I* had in mind for me. But since I ditched school, I
have always supported myself—sometimes marginally,
but always honestly. I have my flaws, but who doesn't?

Am I really a complete disappointment? The human equivalent of a rained-out baseball game, or a Mick Jagger solo record?

There is an old joke: The first female president of the United States is being sworn in on the steps of the Capitol. The first female *Jewish* president. Her mother is sitting in the audience, beaming. She turns to the person next to her and says, "You see that woman up there? The one with her hand on the Bible? Her brother is a doctor." Some people are just never satisfied.

Getting hired as the publisher of *High Times* magazine, what my grandma always called "that dope rag," was (to continue hammering at the *2001* metaphor) like "Project Jupiter," a mission that went farther out into space then humans had ever gone before, but one that was ultimately doomed to fail. Nonetheless, it was the apex of my career, and between my salary and the bonus money I got for boosting ad sales, plus the dough I was socking away from a couple of sordid writing gigs I was hustling on the side (a lot of kayfabe letters for *Penthouse*, which, once upon a time, paid very decent money for fabulized first-person sex tales), I was able to put a down payment on a Manhattan apartment.

My mother was thrilled that I was buying my first home, and she brought me a huge box of nonstick cookware as a housewarming gift. My father wasn't as impressed. He hated New York City—he thought it was "filthy" and didn't understand why anyone would want to live there. Dad was unflinching in his opinion that buying an apartment there was not a *mitzvah*, but a *mistake*.

After about four years, that job went south—the confluence of my ultimate inability to shepherd a staff of stoners without fomenting revolt, and the crashing of New York's media economy after the terror attacks of September 11. It was a rough time, with not a lot of publishing jobs available for forty-year-olds with high salary requirements who had already decided how the world was supposed to be run. Jobs were especially not forthcoming for those whose last résumé entries were pot, porn, and professional wrestling. As one potential employer sniffed, "That's not a résumé, that's a crime scene."

I was paying my mortgage with my credit card to avoid completely bleeding out my bank account—a genuinely terrible idea—but somehow I managed to keep things rolling and just kept pressing forward. I got a few cherry gigs writing press releases and liner notes for old-school punk rockers (the Stooges, the New York Dolls, the Ramones), but as usual, downtime turned out to be the greatest blessing: I managed to get in the studio and make a new record, the first one with me on vocals and guitar, which led to about forty gigs in France and a new and sizable affection for drinking calvados. I did another tour of Spain, back on drums with my old band. I even worked as a professional wrestler for a hot second, taking a time-keeper's bell to the face in my ring debut in Strasbourg (it took twenty-seven stitches to sew me up—no kayfabe, totally legit), all of which became the viscous narrative of my first book. Somehow, just being myself and working hard had earned me a spiffy publishing deal. My father would have lost that bet. I should have given him odds.

Right around the same time I landed a good freelance gig doctoring rock bios and memoirs. Apparently, being a musician and an author made me uniquely qualified. I enjoyed it. I was good at it—I worked on books with guys who had played with Frank Zappa, John Lennon, and Bob Dylan, to name but a few—and I was eventually offered a job running the desk. It lasted right up until the Solstice of Suck.

The job was a real plum, editing and polishing classic rock bios and histories, with occasional flights into jazz and country (and punk rock, when I thought I could get away with it). Among my favorites was a prog-rock coffee table book for stoners—a topic that I hardly hold dear, but how much fun was it choosing pictures of men in silver capes huddled over ridiculously complex synthesizer banks, swaddled in purple smoke from the dry ice machine? It was *anti*-punk and, therefore, *punker* than punk. Or at least that's what I told myself at the time.

Within a year I had paid down my credit card bill and had a long-term plan in place (for a change): to hang on to this job and, like at the end of *2001*, eventually evolve into the next level of human consciousness, which apparently was some sort of omniscient star child.

The last book I did for them, *Reconsidering Yoko Ono*, was with one of my favorite writers and artists, Lisa Carver. The idea was inspired as much by Pete Hamill's book *Why Sinatra Matters*—which more or less lives in my bathroom—as it was by a genuine desire to see a thoughtful treatment of Yoko as an artist and not simply as the yellow menace that busted up the Beatles. I was thrilled that Lisa was on board with the idea, and the book was eventually excerpted by the *New York Times Magazine*—a coup of no uncertain magnitude. I said to her at the time that if this were the last book I ever worked on, I'd be very proud. I didn't mean it literally, though, and I was let go the day it came out. Who knows—maybe it was a conspiracy by paranoid Beatles fans, still up in arms that she led John over to the dark side of the avant-garde. No matter, I was out of a job.

WHEN MY CAT DIED, the world lost a great spirit, and I lost a great friend. Manly, "The World's Strongest Cat," was a cat greater than his race. When he entered a room, it was like ten cats came into the room. More than nine lives, he lived a thousand. His spirit was indomitable.

Manly got his nickname a year or so after we began our journey together. He had a boo-boo on his ear, so I took him to see Dr. Ted, who had been our friend and trusted veterinarian since I rescued him (the cat, that is—not the doctor) after he had been abandoned by an East Village bodega. "Well," Dr. Ted said, "I can lance it, but I'd rather cut his ear and clean it and stitch it. Then it'll never happen again. I see this all the time. His ear will be a little bent over when we're done, but . . ."

But cute as hell! Women *swooned* over that ear. After I saw it I thought about having it done myself.

Anyway, I was supposed to leave Manly at the doctor's office in the early morning and pick him up in the evening, but at noon my phone rang.

"Mike, you have to come get your cat."

"Huh?"

"Well, usually an eyedropper's worth of anesthesia will do the trick, but Manly wasn't going for it. We had to shoot him up like a German shepherd. And then he should have been asleep for twenty hours, but the second I got done stitching him he woke up and went for the food. You really need to come get him; he is making the other animals look bad. He is the strongest animal we have ever seen."

Oh boy, was I ever *kvelling*!

And he was such a good pal, too, although he was the worst wingman imaginable. He was just too good-looking and charismatic.

About ten years after he was crowned World's Strongest Cat, Manly became very sick. I thought he was going to die. One day he woke up bleeding from his nose, and one of his eyes was swollen shut. I wrapped him in a blanket and took him to the emergency room. He needed a blood transfusion and a few days' stay in the hospital, and against the prognosis of everyone there he made a full comeback. While he was in the hospital he had a team of gorgeous female doctors and nurses attending to him, and he was an incredible flirt, batting his one good eye at every pretty girl in the hospital—and they all fell apart when he did, like cookies being dunked in milk.

When he left the hospital, there was a line of knockout animal health-care experts, all showing just a little too much leg and blowing kisses at him like he was Elvis Presley on his way to the army: "Good-bye Manly! Good luck, Manly!" I swear one nurse tried to give him her phone number.

He had lost a lot of weight—seven pounds, which is a lot even for a big cat like Manly—but he put it right back on, like Robert De Niro in *Raging Bull*. If he had a chance to claim purchase on a stray piece of turkey or roast beef, you would have done well to get out of his way. When it came to victuals, Manly was simply not to be fucked with.

Sometime after that, he had an ugly carbuncle on his side that required surgery. Again, leave the cat in the morning, pick him up in the evening.

As if.

At noon, the phone rang.

"Mike, come get your cat . . . He's awake and making fun of the other cats."

In the background I heard the nurse, who had (unsurprisingly) fallen in love with Manly, say, "Tell Mike he's doing push-ups now!"

There are more Manly stories. He loved music. When I played the guitar, he plucked at the strings, and when I fooled with the little Casiotone keyboard that I had bought with every intention of learning how to play the piano, he would leap up onto it to show me how it was done. He was a very aggressive, very dedicated avant-gardist, seemingly setting up twelve tone rows willy-nilly and improvising wildly. Finally I begged him, "Why can't you just play one fucking flatted seventh, or a goddam minor chord for a change?" His reaction was to fling my phone across the room like a supermodel.

Ah, the phone flinging. His favorite trick, right before flinging the keys, the remote control, and my sunglasses.

It had gotten to the point where I felt like it was my fault if I left any of the above in the Hot Zone—namely, on top of the kitchen table—even for a moment. He'd jump on the table, look me straight in the eyes, and *shwoop!* There went the phone. *Shwoop!* Sunglasses under the couch. I can't tell you how much time I spent looking for my keys thanks to his kittenish pranksterism, even when I wasn't stoned.

Speaking of making eye contact, it was a big part of his charm. He always made you feel like you were the most important one in the relationship. He was often compared to Bill Clinton that way. He could slay anyone.

In his final days, he withered but was still the life of the party. A somewhat cantankerous but lovable old man, he'd punch me in the nose playfully every morning, demanding the early seating for breakfast. He was eighteen years old, and when he went, he went quickly, bravely letting me know it was time.

How lucky am I to have been his best buddy and caretaker? While it broke my heart into pieces, I feel strong that my final act for him was the greatest act of love and compassion I could possibly do for my friend, The World's Strongest Cat.

Soon after Fortuna spun her wheel downward, my brother called to say, "I heard you lost your job, sorry about that," adding after a long beat, "I'm sorry about your cat, too." Another beat. "But not as much as your job." My mother was sad to hear about my job, too. No word on the cat or the girlfriend. Regarding my father, she told me to "get over it." These were not sentimental people, but they had their priorities.

And that was the basic architecture of the Summer of Suck.

GENERALLY, I AM EXPERT at keeping my life in a reasonably stress-free zone. Mostly it's pretty easy: I don't worry when worrying doesn't help. I don't panic at deadlines, I work toward them. I don't get caught up in juvenile gossip and bullshit. I try to bend in the wind, not snap. I laugh out loud every day. But weeks after he died, my father's words hung in the air like a particularly smug version of the Ghost of Christmas Past—"disappointment," "failure," "broken." What the fuck was wrong with me? My stock had bottomed out: Edison Preferred was in the toilet with no takers. I was a middle-aged, unemployed, single guy living alone with his cat.

And then the cat up and died. It was truly pathetic.

That the cat had been my most successful long-term relationship was itself a sad statement, but after almost twenty years together, his death punched a black-hole-like singularity in the landscape—I had enjoyed many more conversations with him than I had with either of my parents, after all. Whether the devastating series of events spoke to my shortcomings as a human or was just an unfortunate run of luck, it didn't seem to matter because, you know, "loser," "failure," "broken" . . . In his last moments, Dad had done some real damage, putting the final, needling touches on a lifetime of hurt. It was his masterpiece: a symphony of pain.

I KNEW RIGHT AWAY that I was experiencing what is commonly known as an "anxiety attack"—what Thomas McGuane once described as "a sudden loss of cabin pressure." I woke up gasping, feeling like I had been body-slammed by a behemoth. Sometimes I dream about professional wrestling, but this wasn't that. Even though I had never actually experienced a full-fledged anxiety attack, I knew all the symptoms. It felt like my soul was being flushed down the toilet. It was the logical extension of living in post-modern America.

Maybe the old man was right. Maybe I was a zero, as evidenced by my empty bed and my dwindling bank account. No matter how good I was at helping aging rock stars find the *mot juste* in their memoirs, or taking my girl out on a sexy dinner date, I was obdurate and just plain stupid when it came to seeing the oncoming storm. Sunshine turned to rain, and there I was: the chump without an umbrella. My once swank bachelor pad had turned into a killing field where bad choices went to die. Within a few weeks I was on a therapist's couch—the last Jewish guy in New York City to have turned that trick.

I tried to imagine what seeing a shrink was going to be like, and all I could think of were movie and television psychiatrists. The whole thing seemed fairly ridiculous: Dr. Bob Hartley on *The Bob Newhart Show*; Dr. Bellows, the thorn in Major Nelson's paw on *I Dream of Jeannie*; Dr. Frasier Crane (and his insufferable but funnier brother); the A-Team of uptight psychoanalysts in *Spellbound*; and my favorite comic-strip Freudian, Lucy van Pelt, with her five-cent solutions.

As it turned out, the therapist I began seeing was more like Dr. Melfi, Tony Soprano's leggy psychiatrist in *The Sopranos*. She was just a couple of years older than me, very smart, and also very warm. As luck would have it, Dr. Headshrinker (as I have come to affectionately call her, with her permission, of course) was also a lapsed wrestling fan, meaning that she'd watched it on TV with her brothers when she was a kid and even harbored some lingering affection for the Junkyard Dog. She made me feel comfortable enough to cry in our first hour together.

I'll confess to having been a little bit nervous. I think that I was afraid I would come out of her office more nuts than I went in. Maybe I'd turn into a neurotic jerk—the punk rock version of Woody Allen, whose entire career seemed predicated on seeing a psychiatrist. He hadn't been funny in years—a fate far worse than death.

The only advice I got when it came to seeing a shrink was to be completely honest. Be yourself, don't hold back—otherwise, it won't work (or, as one Jewish friend put it, you won't get your money's worth). Seeing as being myself was pretty much what got me there in the first place, it didn't seem like too much to ask.

I told her the story of my dad's last homily, that I was feeling overwhelmed by life, and that, for the first time that I could remember, I was having trouble coping. I felt like my integrity (if nothing else) was still intact, but at middle age I thought I would be a lot further ahead in my life and career. I was starting to think that my father was right to suggest that there was something seriously wrong with me.

"You are who you want to be, not who he told you to be," she reassured me. "And let me tell you, this story could have ended a lot differently. Men come in here every day and tell me about fathers who bullied them, who told them all their lives that they were stupid. Women, too. Really great, smart individuals grew up thinking they were stupid and worthless because that's what their fathers told them their whole lives. They wind up failing in college and in their marriages, drowning in self-doubt. Then, when they are forty or fifty, they realize that they were pretty bright after all. Like you, they are over-whelmed with conflicting emotions: They wanted to love their fathers but never got the chance because their fathers were bullies. The story doesn't always end so well—there are a lot of guys who don't make it as far as my office.

"Listen," she told me, practically leveling me, "he sabotaged you. When he bought you broken drums and then yelled at you for not playing them, he set you up for failure and then blamed you for it. Every time *you* showed some talent that he didn't have—taking pictures, what-ever—he tried to suppress it. He had to be in control. Even when he was dying, he had to remind you that he was somehow still in control. He had to win. It's the classic sign of a narcissistic father."

"Well, yeah," I conceded. "But it's not like he beat me up or anything . . ."

"What are you talking about? That's exactly what he did."

"A poor little middle-class Jewish boy singing the blues seems pretty fucking weak. 'My Daddy didn't love me enough,' and here I am whining about it. I think I should be over it."

I apologized for cussing, but she told me not to worry about it; she did it all the time. I was starting to like Dr. Headshrinker.

"But how did the old man become such a pill?" I asked her, because every monster needs its origin story. I'd settle for a benign creation myth. I felt like an explanation would go a long way to helping me find some peace.

"Well, you're the writer. Maybe you can figure it out, why he was like he was. Did his parents show him love and support?"

"They were cold. His father was browbeaten by his mother, who always thought that she had married down. Her father came from Russia with some money—he had won the Irish lottery, come to America, and started a successful paper business selling boxes, industrial cardboard, paper towels, and whatnot. My dad's mom had six sisters, and the legend was that they came from Russian royalty, but that was complete bullshit. Nonetheless, that was the story they told. So my dad's family was kayfabing for at least two generations. Maybe that's where he got it—I have no idea. Anyway, they had enough family money to buy this terrific house and send the kids to shmancy private schools and everything else. My dad's father got a job in his father-in-law's business, selling toilet paper or something awful, but they were pretty well set."

"That goes a long way to explaining why your father wouldn't want to be like his dad. But it doesn't give him license to be mean to his children. Nothing does. How did he treat your brothers? The same as you?"

"Not at all. I think he was still fairly emotionally remote, but he was certainly more present in their lives, encouraging their decisions. But they took the straight and narrow, you know: One became a lawyer; the other one is a very successful financial guy. Their experience was much different. Me, I couldn't do anything right."

"And how do they treat their kids?"

"Incredibly well. They love their kids. If anything, they spoil them. Beats the alternative, right? I guess being a dick to your kids skips a generation, or something . . ."

"It's different when you are the firstborn. Also, they were conformists, and you weren't. They provided a narrative he could understand."

"He used to tell me, really angry, 'You chose a tough road to go down, pal. It could have been a lot different.'"

"He actually called you 'pal'?"

"Yeah, I hated that. I never knew what to make of it . . . but the point here is that my life could have been a lot easier if I had just been, I don't know, someone else?"

"The point is that *he* could have made your life better. *He* was in control and could have taken care of you, if you did exactly what *he* said. That was the price."

"Well, that wasn't going to happen. But the big question is: Don't you think by this point in my life I shouldn't be hung up on my father? It's pretty fucked up. I am starting to think that it's entirely possible that he was right: I'm failing at life because I have been making a series of bad decisions. On the other hand, maybe I'm a loser because 'failure' has been so ingrained in me that it's what I've become. He told me my whole life that I would never make it, and after a few modest successes, maybe now I am just regressing to the mean, as they say."

"What failure? If you had listened to him you never would have played the drums, traveled, written a book— anything. You've had this amazing life."

She had a point, of course. But months after that scene in the hospital room, I still heard his voice everywhere I went. Looking in the mirror, shaving: "You are broken and need to be fixed." Sitting at the kitchen table, writing: "No one wants to read your shit." Walking down the street, on the way to see Dr. Headshrinker: "You are a complete disappointment." The anxiety attack had sealed it: The guy had really gotten under my skin.

"Basically," I told her, considering my career right up until that point, including my last anemic royalty statement, my current employment status, and the precarious mystery of how I was going to pay for this session, "I have a bright future behind me."

She laughed, because she is very kind, adding, "It's a good thing you came to see me."

5

HOW TO WIN FRIENDS AND INFLUENCE IDIOTS

Y ou would have liked my father if you had met him. He was, as we say in the wresting business, "a good worker," meaning he knew how to "work the crowd." He knew how to put himself "over." Perhaps I'm being cynical, not to mention pretty damn cheeky, using slang from his least favorite industry in the world to describe him. *Mon petit vengeance!*

But wrestling has always served as a great metaphor for life. It has never failed me—at least not yet.

My father was very successful. He made a lot of money, which he obsessed over and which, of course, was his yardstick for others' success as well. He was by all accounts a great businessman, tops in his field, developing a thriving office and retail space in northern New Jersey.

I was in awe of his acumen, and I had a ton of respect for anyone who made it like he did, through hard work and a fair degree of vision. He began as a commercial real estate salesman and was so good at it that they gave him a piece of the company. He was an admired executive, popular with his colleagues and peers, and much lauded in the local business press. Such was his reputation that by the time I was just getting out of high school, he was named CEO of a major development. The guy was a titan in his industry. The buildings he worked on are still there—a testament to his drive. It's his legacy, like a pyramid, except that people go there to work in cubicles and get their nails done and gossip by the watercooler.

Dad was a student of the Dale Carnegie school, literally sleeping with his copy of *How to Win Friends and Influence People*. It was ever-present, tucked into a headboard-cum-bookcase, the kind of modern-esque 1970s bedroom design that was intended to elevate the boudoir into something pragmatic and ergonomic. Looking back, it was actually a lot like the veneered build-it-yourself furniture you can get for less than two hundred dollars at Ikea® these days, but back then it was a custom job—"custom" being the prime shibboleth for good taste in suburban shelving back then, sort of like how track lighting was once considered *très* sophisticated.

On his side of the bed were his books, including the Dale Carnegie Baedeker. Next to that was Alvin Toffler's *Future Shock*, a treatise on information overload and rapidly advancing technology that was also very popular at the time. I read it cover to cover—it seems quaint now, but Toffler was definitely on to something. I was as much attracted by the title (which sounded like a cool science-fiction movie) as I was by the idea that reading one of my dad's favorite books would bring us closer together.

It did not.

I understood it probably as well as any twelve-year-old ever would. I particularly liked the parts about mass production and disposable goods, since that jibed pretty well with my own fear of a future dominated by landfills in New Jersey and Staten Island and it pretty much validated my bar mitzvah speech, which I don't think he was too keen on, either. But in terms of fostering a conversation with the old man, it was all worth *bupkus*.

Incongruously, next to *Future Shock* was his well-worn copy of *Jonathan Livingston Seagull*, which, if you recall, was a treacly, spiritual-cum-self-help novella whose incredible popularity at the time was a perfect example of hypocritical middle-class squares adopting a soft-pedaled hippie homily to help convince themselves that they were somehow enlightened, despite being on the wrong side of everything in the 1960s. It was genuinely among the dumbest, most banal things I had ever read (if "reading" is even an accurate description of how one absorbed this sort of gobbledygook)—just completely lame in every possible way—and it left me wondering how I could possibly be the progeny of the kind of people who kept this sort of brainless crud next to their beds. This was what passed for wisdom among hapless squares?

Meanwhile, on my mother's side of the bed were the hotted-up, best-selling bodice rippers of the day: Jackie Collins, Harold Robbins, and the like. Jacqueline Susann would have been a bit too hip, although Erica Jong's *Fear of Flying* had somehow found its way in there. I have no idea if any of its implicit messages of second-wave feminism and sexual freedom resonated with her. I am guessing not.

In between Mom and Dad, in a cubbyhole that also held a box of tissues and a squeeze bottle of store-brand hand cream, were popular self-help titles—*I'm OK, You're OK* (some hooey about "transactional analysis" that my otherwise precocious brain could not possibly parse) and Gail Sheehy's *Passages* (about the "predictable crises of adult life," which promised to be a tour de force of the arc of human existence). I found *Passages* not so much incomprehensible as just boring, but then again, I was only twelve years old and an entire lifetime away from the "Forlorn 40s—Dangerous years when the dreams of youth demand reassessment, men and women switch characteristics, sexual panic is common, but the greatest opportunity for self-discovery awaits." What the fuck did I know? The adults who owned the copy were in the midst of the shaken illusions of the "Catch 30s"—in 1976 Mom was thirty-six and Dad was thirty-nine—and presumably able to glom something from it, even if the "self-discovery" promised after the "sexual panic" came in the form of a grueling, hopelessly bitter divorce.

As for the men and women switching characteristics, not a chance. As things got worse between them, they only became more trenchant, with their own worst characteristics amplified logarithmically. It was amazing to consider that they had ever been able to have a civil conversation, let alone procreate. They each quickly remarried with a minimum of fanfare or romance, somehow finding people remarkably suited to themselves: My mom married a milquetoast accountant who held precious few skills when it came to conversation but could swing a golf club, and perhaps as important held no opinion of her taste for animal-print wallpaper and designer handbags. My dad's new wife simply adopted his gimmick of studied preppy perfection and self-consciously humble affluence. Sometimes it seemed as if they were all part of some sociological experiment in middle-aged coupling where husband and wife eventually begin to resemble each other physically.

Not improbably, my father didn't invite his children to his second wedding, preferring to let us know at his first convenience after the fact ("we got married on Cape Cod a few weeks ago"), while my mom invited *only* her children and took pictures of us in her driveway, like a low-rent senior prom.

SPEAKING OF THE BODICE RIPPERS, the kind of literary junk food my mom read, I want to tell you a story about what I like to call "the cocaine penis."

I read a lot back then, as always. Anything that was in the house I gave a look-see. There wasn't really a lot to explore aside from the books in the bedroom (not counting my father's not-so-well-hidden copy of *The Joy of Sex*, one of the early editions with the drawings of hippies with massive, tangled forests of pubic hair). A few stray books were pushed into a corner downstairs—stuff obviously left over from previous lives that no one had the heart to throw out: a couple of art books that my father had bought in college and my mother's childhood copy of *Alice in Wonderland*, which I claimed as my own more or less the same day I discovered marijuana. I still have it.

Anyway, about the cocaine penis. I'm pretty sure it was in Arthur Hailey's book *The Moneychangers*, which

I found sitting on the kitchen table, waiting to be taken back to the library. Driven by teenage intellectual ennui and prurient curiosity, I just picked it up and started thumbing through it, and that's when I stumbled upon the cocaine penis—and my literary life was forever changed.

It was the single most lurid scene I have ever read, anywhere, still to this day, and this coming from a guy who went on to write literally dozens of pornographic novels and hundreds of sex scenes (first-time lesbian housewife confessions were my specialty in the early 1990s). For a thirteen-year-old boy, this shit was just *beyond.*

I suppose I owe it to myself (and to you, dear reader, who will want every gooey detail) to go out and find a copy of this mind-warping bit of perversion, but working from my memory—where it is pretty well engraved—the gist is that one of those master-of-the-universe-type banking hotshots, the kind of financier who lives in a virtual cloud city far away from us mortals, was having a high time with his high-paid hooker, splayed on his arena-sized rotating bed. And just when it seemed like he couldn't possibly be having a better time, he whips out a vial of cocaine and somehow fashions a sparkly line of the stuff on his erect penis. I have no recollection of what happened next—which orifice he stuck it in, or how this brought him pleasure, since cocaine is basically a numbing agent. Perhaps it was for her benefit? My eyes got all screwy just reading the words. My brain reeled. I couldn't believe that somewhere in my mother's mind, for the rest of her entire life, was a giant, tumescent penis, fili-greed with a sparkling line of freshly ground disco dust.

Relative to *Jonathan Livingston Seagull*, at least there was some heat in this thing. But more significantly, this was my first clue that it was all a charade—everyone had dark secrets and dirty thoughts, stuff they couldn't or wouldn't do in public, but incubated in their heads.

Later I would pay tribute to the cocaine penis's sin-gular squalor by including a similar scene in every single one of the twenty-eight pornographic novels I wrote in the 1980s. If you ever find yourself reading a cheap sex novel from the era, no matter what name is given to the author, and stumble upon a scene with someone putting cocaine on their erection, it is probably my work.

But I digress.

To most people who knew my father, at least casually or professionally, he was considered a genuinely nice guy. But this is my story. I have no doubt that if he wrote this book, I would be the villain.

DAD HAD BEEN SICKER than anyone short of his wife or his doctor had known. He had multiple myeloma—

a cancer of plasma cells that is considered treatable but ultimately incurable—and he had it for many years. I didn't know about it until about two years after he died, when I began research for this book. When I asked my brothers if they knew how Dad died, they didn't. I got vague answers. *An infection? Something with his lungs?*

The cancer was a well-guarded secret, even after his death, which is its own kind of wrong: Adult children have a right to know their parents' medical history. One of the first questions the doctor asks is if there is any history of cancer in the family, and for a long time we were all giving the wrong answer.

If he wanted to kayfabe his health, honestly, I respect that. You never heard the slightest hint of "woe-is-me" from him. Stoicism is a very admirable trait. Some might even say he was brave.

His wife finally told me the truth, adding, "You know your father, he had to be perfect. He didn't want anyone to see him as anything besides perfect." In the end, his lungs had become infected, and that's what killed him. The radiation treatments he had begun receiving to fight the cancer had punished his immune system to the point where he couldn't fight back.

Perhaps it was a lack of theology or spirituality, or just simply his obsession with success, but my Dad saw mortality as a glitch in his gimmick and as a weakness in other people. Thinking that he could outrun it did him no good in the end.

I don't know much about dying, but I figure if you know it's breathing down your neck, it might be a good time to make your peace with God and, maybe, your loved ones—at the very least, yourself—because that has got to beat hands-down twirling off into the unknown pissed off and leaving a legacy of hurt. At that point the kayfabe is all over. No more gimmick. It's as real as it fucking gets.

When my father was admitted to the hospital for what turned out to be his final visit, Brother No. 1 told him, "You need to let Michael know. He'll want to come see you," to which Dad responded, "No, he needs to call me, and don't you tell him that I said that, either."

"You don't want me to let him know that you are in the hospital?"

"No. If he cared, he would call me."

At that point, Brother No. 1 stuck up for me. "You do understand why he hasn't called, don't you? Because the last time we were all together you told him in front of the entire family to shut the fuck up, no one gives a shit what he thinks, and that he isn't as smart as he thinks he is. You also called him fat. You can't really blame him." With that, he went rogue and called me to tell me the story, prefacing it with "you can't tell Dad I called you, he told me not to."

Even now, I find it hard to believe my father was in a hospital dying, and he actually made an effort to keep it a secret from me. If Brother No. 1 had taken his marching orders from the old man, it was very possible I would have never seen him again. I suppose I could have stayed away, all things considered, but I was still holding out for some sort of approval—a star in the sky, any goddam thing. I needed a signal. At forty-something years old, it still hurt too much to give up on our relationship, no matter how slashing and caustic his comments had become. This was not the moment to terminate our relationship for the rest of eternity; this was our opportunity to come together and heal. We still had time.

So I called Dad to say, "Hi, I was thinking of coming to visit on Father's Day with Brother No. 1." Without missing a beat—lacking any sign of emotional cacophony or hurt feelings or former fights—he beamed, "Oh, that would be great, I would love to see you," and in fact he had a case of Stags' Leap Cabernet—did I know what that was? It was a gift from one of his fabulously rich friends, and he would love to share it with me. "Sure," I say, "that would be great." Everything was ducky.

I met my brother at the airport and we went straight over to the hospital to see the old man. This was the day before the Great Deathbed Litany. When we got to the hospital, he seemed happy enough to see me, but I hardly had a chance to give him a kiss and say hello, or get a grip on the dizzying lattice of IV tubes and wires spraying in all directions from under his toothpaste-green hospital gown, and just how freaking gaunt he was—his face was the color of sour milk, and he looked like he had lost fifty pounds since the last time I saw him—before he began with his specialty, the small talk. Innocently enough—or so it seemed—he started a conversation about the current spate of so-called sex scandals, based on a story in the *New York Times*, which was lying open on the bedside tray.

This was right in my wheelhouse, and I offered the opinion that all sex scandals were not created equal: Some behavior was perhaps immoral, but certainly not illegal; other "scandals" were not really scandalous at all—just sensational, say between two unmarried and consenting adults, but one is a celebrity or there is a large age difference. But who was I to judge?

Mostly people just hate hypocrites. If you were that guy in the US Senate screaming the loudest about family values and demanding to see Bill Clinton's head on a pike when he got caught dallying with the intern, it might have been best if you didn't get snagged with your own dick in the cookie jar. And when the closeted, self-loathing hate-mongers who cherry-picked their litany of lunacy from Leviticus got caught cruising men's rooms in Midwest airports, well, it seemed pretty obvious, to me at least, that America was at some sort of pathological odds with its Puritan underpinning, simultaneously fearing sex and running toward it. The filthiest thing I have ever read, after all, was a book that my mom had taken out of a small-town library.

"You don't know what you are talking about," I was told. "Anyway, no one wants your opinion."

This struck me as somewhat odd, since he had clearly asked me, "Michael, what do you think?" just before trampling all over what I have to consider a thoughtful and studied response. If this were the kind of bullshit that he wanted to perpetrate from his hospital bed within mere moments of my arrival, maybe I should have realized he was just warming up for the main event.

Anyway, that kind of put the kibosh on the whole conversation, since no one else had anything to add after that. There was an awkward silence before he said, "I have that great case of wine back at the house. Stags' Leap. It is *very* expensive." Then he turned to my brother and said, "I want you to have it."

I'm just standing there like our old friend Kaw-Liga, the cigar-store Indian, with really nothing to say, when he turns to me and says, "I have an old watch for you, if you want it. It's a Timex®."

Once upon a time, I learned that when someone offers you a gift, the only gracious response is to accept it. The giving of gifts, like changing for dinner, is one of those niceties that separates us from the animals. More than that, I have learned that the proper *accepting* of gifts is what really constitutes a high level of *menschdom*. Just ask Emily Post: One must never betray one's disappointment with a gift—that is indefensibly *rude*. Feign enthusiasm, and if the gift is a real turd, like an ugly sweater or some old watch that no one wants, you must still say, "I can't wait to use it." Giving and receiving are both gestures whose niceties can be elevated with a bit of disingenuous ardor. And so I said, "Oh, of course! I would love that! In fact, I could really use a new watch. So thank you, thank you very much. That's really great," or words to that effect, only to be cut off at the knees with "if you aren't going to use it, don't take it."

Oy fucking vey, I just can't win with this guy. But I reiterate my enthusiasm, even though we both know that I just got the booby prize—the mule that was standing behind Curtain Number Three—while my brother was going to walk away with twelve bottles of extremely potable if not exceptional wine. And the next day Dad's wife shows up with the watch, and it is, as advertised, an old Timex. But again I take the high road and say what a great watch it is, even though, the moment I get home, it goes straight into my sock drawer to be forgotten.

MY FATHER ALWAYS "WORKED BABYFACE"—which is wrestling parlance for playing the good guy. (The bad guys are called "heels.") But Dad was also adroit at executing what's known as a "heel turn," pivoting from good guy to bad guy, 180 degrees, on a dime. For better or worse, I was probably the only person to ever see it, aside from those lucky family members who got a front-row seat.

That bit in the hospital with the wine and the watch, and baiting me by asking my opinion only to tell me to shut up, was classic stuff. It was a lot like the shtick of the great 1980s heel, the Million Dollar Man, who riled up the audience with stunts like, say, promising a small boy five hundred dollars if he could bounce a basketball fifteen times in a row, only to kick the ball out from under the boy after the fourteenth bounce. He got a lot of "heat," as we say, in that people wanted to kill him. It was a good gimmick in that a lot of tickets were sold to folks who wanted to see him get his ass kicked. But it must have been just my good fortune, getting to see this side of my father. Everyone else, as far as I can tell, got the charming, generous, affable version.

The Dale Carnegie thing is no joke—fifteen million people have read it, and for good reason. It works. *How to Win Friends and Influence People* promises to make you more popular, increase your earnings, make you a better executive, and win people over to your way of thinking. It is a panacea for avoiding conflict and keeping relations smooth, with dozens of bullet points, bromides, and easily mastered psychological sleights of hand, all aimed at making people like you. Warren Buffett and Charles Manson swore by it.

The problem with the Dale Carnegie school, of course, is that it's pure kayfabe. It works great if you're a sales guy. It is a solid course for ambitious executives, Rotary Club leaders, and apparently cult murderers, but it has nothing to do with forming deep or long-lasting relationships— which I guess suited the old man just fine.

Tellingly, in his last moments, my father's best friend in the world—aside from his wife, whose love and loyalty were unflinching, so much that she didn't even throw a flag on the play during his unnecessarily rough Final Beat Down—seemed to be his auto mechanic, a young-looking thirtysomething whom he described to me as "just a really terrific young man." Transient, short-term friendships with people who worked for him had been a constant in the old man's life. The only relationships I ever saw him maintain were either those in which he was in some sort of financial control, or those in which he was in awe of someone else's net worth.

In the relationship department, I am far wealthier than my dad ever was. I am incredibly fortunate to have a large number of close friends, as well as an ever-expanding circle of people whom I am humbled and flattered to know and who intersect with my life in all sorts of interesting ways. Our varying degrees of intimacy and fraternity and disparate strangeness grow and change and ebb and flow, but they have, across decades, endured the crap that life is so expert at serving. Many of my relationships come from the exact choices that Dad had promised would only incubate a life below the poverty line, and which apparently made me such a complete disappointment: I chose to be a writer and a musician and an artist—trades that have fostered many joyous, deeply shared experiences, indelible bonds, and healthy rivalries, and that continue to inject every day with new possibilities and a powerful sense of belonging. Friends, I have heard it said, are like the family you get to choose yourself. Obviously there are circles within circles, and wide variances of personal tastes, to say the least. Some of my friends like stripes, and some like polka dots, but I am pretty sure they all dig the Ramones.

* * *

FOR ALL OF HIS SUCCESS in "winning" friends and influencing people, I did see my father's highly polished affability and small talk backfire at least once.

I was visiting him up on Cape Cod, where he had a house for a while. I had just turned thirty-five and had a terrific job and a swell girlfriend whom I brought with me on that trip, because no matter what—or, at least, that's what I thought back then—a place to stay on Cape Cod was a pretty good deal and should have boosted my net worth in her eyes. As it was, she was appalled.

The house was appointed with the usual *chazerai*—expensive books of local photography, framed nautical charts, etc.—all new and clean and with no real provenance and very little vibe, but just enough money spent to signal reserved and appropriate good taste. Like his other home, not a stitch was out of place, from the highly curated throw pillows to the remote control for the TV, which had its own little nest.

It was a weird place to visit. I felt neither like a guest nor family. There were a lot of rules. I was told I had to shave every day (??), always wear a shirt, and no bare feet in the house *ever*—directives that were clear manifestations of his fear of, I don't know, beach bums? Beatniks?

Then why have a house near the beach and invite your kids up for summer vacation?

What he didn't see coming was that his wife had invited one of her kids to visit at the same time, and he made his entrance in cutoff shorts, no shirt, no shoes, looking a lot like one of the hopped-up hodads in *Beach Blanket Bingo*.

We were all treated equally that week, just some of us more equally than others. Me, I was a clean-shaven man for the duration, padding around the house in socks like Grandma Fucking Moses. No effort was made to buy the other guy a razor, a shirt, or some footwear.

Meanwhile, my father just poured compliments all over this guy. Everything he did was wickedly exciting (he was going on and on about some home electronics project), while I was subtly put down with indifference the entire weekend. It was about par for the course. I guess I had gotten used to it, but the girlfriend was plainly disgusted.

"How do you stand it? Listening to his crap?"

"It isn't so bad," I protested.

"What the fuck are you talking about? He treats everyone around him like his best pal. Everyone is awesome, except for you. He was more interested in where the waiter at dinner last night went to school than in anything you had had to say. And *home electronics*? I mean, *seriously.*"

I realized then that my stock was plummeting. I looked weak.

The real *shpilkes* began one early evening when we were rolling out of his driveway, Dad and his wife in the front seat, girlfriend and me in the back, when he pulled up next to the couple in the house next door who were busy taking out the garbage. Ostensibly he just wanted to say hi to his neighbors, which is what people did up there. Island etiquette and all that. Everyone spent so much time waving to one another I'm surprised there wasn't an outbreak of carpal tunnel syndrome.

That he didn't see any problem with slow-rolling up to strangers in his SUV and asking them where they lived, that maybe it would not be seen as a friendly gesture, was the first problem. That they happened to be an African American couple in a notoriously white New England enclave did not help.

To be fair, Dad introduced himself first and said, "Hi, we live next door . . ." But it didn't matter. The couple looked positively mortified, even as they forced smiles and introduced themselves and said, "Uh, hi. We're staying here, in this house . . ."

Satisfied that everything was in order, Dad turned on his charm.

"Is this your first wife or your second?" he teased the fellow.

My girlfriend was livid. I tried unsuccessfully to use a Jedi mind trick to vanish into the ether. Meanwhile, the poor guy forced a smile and said, "First wife. Thirty years."

Dad said something like "nice to meet you and have a nice evening" and continued down the street. Driving away, I mentioned that maybe that wasn't too cool and that if he found himself in need of a cup of flour, maybe I wouldn't go knocking on their door—that bird had flown.

"You are *wrong*," he told me very flatly, almost aggressively, which kind of made me think he knew that he fucked up, but he wasn't backing off. "You don't know what you are talking about. We were just having fun."

That night, the girlfriend told me she wanted to go back home. "I was so embarrassed," she fumed. "He seemed like he was giving them the once-over, like he was the neighborhood watch. And that joke about second wives? Is that what rich Jewish people on Cape Cod think is funny? Because my parents are old-school Catholic and don't believe in divorce and if they had heard that shit they would have been like, morally, *righteously* offended. Who the fuck does he think he is that he can just say anything that pops into his head to anyone?"

Later she told me that if we broke up, I should never, ever introduce him to future girlfriends; he was a liability. We broke up—horribly—and I kept her advice. But even after all of that, I still thought that maybe, just *maybe*, it was *me* who had the problem.

6

"YOU BUILT A COMPUTER WHEN YOU WERE EIGHT, AND THEN . . . NOTHING!!"

Mike, why are you still blaming yourself? His expectations were impossible to meet, and when you didn't meet them—and there was no way that you ever could—he marginalized you. He belittled you every chance he got. It's like a laundry list for the narcissistic father. He was competitive with you. He pitted you against your mom. He denied you your individuality. You have a strong sense of values—you believe very strongly in what is right and what is wrong— and he mocked you for it. He had no empathy for you. What did he say when you told him you broke up with your first girlfriend?"

"He said, 'So what? Your mother broke up with me.'"

"How old were you?"

"Thirteen."

"What an asshole."

"Are mental health professionals supposed to say things like that?"

"If it helps. Did he ever say to call him if you needed him? Even when you were a kid, when your parents first got divorced?"

"No."

"So when he wasn't being mean, he was being indifferent. He gaslit you into thinking you were a failure. What more do you need to know? You came in here practically drowning in self-doubt, even though by any standard you are successful."

"Well, I don't know about that. I'm not even close to where I think I should be in my career. And I still don't speak French."

"Mike, you figured out a way to make a living doing what you love to do. Your father did everything in his power to stop you. What did you write in your book about why you dropped out of college?"

"I wrote that I flagged out because I was 'neither hard working nor humble enough.' Which was very honest."

"It may well have been, but that isn't the entire story. Why were you trying to protect him? He tried to sabotage you. You are actually extremely motivated. He's the one that fucked up, not you. And then he scapegoated you for his failure."

It's true. He always told me that I needed to grow the hell up and stop blaming him for my failure at college. And when I wrote my first memoir I thought maybe— just *maybe*—he would read it. Never mind the tawdry topics of punk rock, pro wrestling, and sex on Spanish beaches—some of his least favorite things, although I don't know how *anyone* could dislike the latter—he would see that I owned my successes *and* my failures and that I could take responsibility for my own destiny. Hopefully he would see that this writing thing had some legs after all. I was forty years old and still desperate for him to like me, even though I was still very angry and wounded. Forty years of browbeating was one thing, but he was so confident in my inability to succeed that he wanted to wager on it? That really stuck with me. The urge to impress him and prove that I was not a failure was very powerful.

But it didn't really work out that way. He claimed to have read my book. "I'm amazed that someone who dropped out of college even knows how to write," he said. I asked him about the part where I talk about leaving college the first time, that whole "hard work and humility" thing. "I must have missed that," he spat.

Oh well, one tries.

* * *

WHEN I WAS ACCEPTED into New York University's film school and they sent me a package with information and applications for all the related scholarship programs and work-study jobs that I may have been eligible for, he threw them all out with an angry swoop. "I told you, if you got in, I would take care of it!" he snapped. I'm not quite sure where the anger came from, but I knew how ridiculously fortunate I was to have that opportunity in the first place. I have many flaws, but one of them, I like to think, is not any misplaced sense of entitlement. Usually I have to fight for whatever I want. Nothing ever comes easy.

I arrived at NYU with a safety pin holding my glasses together, and trust me: This wasn't any sort of punk rock statement or some advanced nerd chic—I just needed new glasses.

It had been a rough summer, what with Dad's constant braying, "It's a waste of time, you'll never make it," and Mom's slightly more benign "I wish you would go to school for something you could use!" When I needed anything for school, like glasses that weren't broken, she'd say, "Tell your father, he doesn't give me any money." And then Dad would say, "Bullshit, ask your mother. She is supposed to take care of you." They had unwittingly

become co-conspirators in a perfect storm of anger, repu-
diation, and willful neglect.

When September finally arrived, he dropped me off
at the dorm with all of my stuff—and I mean literally *all
of my stuff*, because I knew I was never going back home.
I had my drums (somewhere along the line I had found
some sticks and was still at it); my entire record collection; my big-ass hi-fi cobbled together from cheap, mostly
used components (Pioneer® receiver, Realistic® tape deck,
BIC® turntable, and giant Advent® speakers, all bought
with money earned at after-school jobs); and a duffel bag
of old clothes (back-to-school sales hadn't been on the
agenda). The other freshmen looked at me as if the circus
wagon had just rolled up.

Everyone was very fresh and crisp. It was a big day.
Parents beamed as they unloaded their Volvos®. Even the
punk rockers were polished up nice and bright—new
Converse® Chucks or spiffy Dr. Martens®, sharp haircuts,
Ramones or Exploited T-shirts torn expertly to varying
degrees of urban suave, depending on one's commitment
to the cause. And everyone had smart-looking mini boom
boxes to play cassettes, or small stereos with automatic
turntables and foldout speakers (such was the technology in 1982), all brand-new.

Most folks could carry their entire record collections
under their arms, which they did very self-consciously

so everyone could see where they staked themselves on the continuum of good taste. There was a lot of Bruce Springsteen and Billy Joel among the jocks, and a lot of new wave and dance music flashed by pretty girls and gay boys who, like me, seemed thrilled to have somehow escaped their suburban nightmare. The Psychedelic Furs were popular that year. I had three crates of records, including lots of punk rock, old blues, a shit ton of jazz, and hard rock—but no classical back then. And definitely no Billy Joel.

The next day I realized that I needed to buy books. I didn't have a credit card or any real cash—I think I only had about fifty bucks left over from my summer job. Classes started that week, and so I called my father to let him know what I would need. Dad told me flatly, "I'm done paying for you. I've had enough." Some parents might be thrilled if their son got into what was probably the East Coast's most prestigious film school. He acted as if I had joined a motorcycle gang.

So I got a job right away to make some money to buy some books, but I was losing traction from the very first day. It was at least a week until I was able to buy any, and by then I was already way behind and off balance. I had a very hard time getting my footing and catching up. When I called Dad to tell him the cafeteria would be closed for a week around Christmas and I needed some money to eat, he told me it wasn't *his* problem—he had already paid enough—and then he promptly fucked off for Cape Cod with his wife. I was not invited. My mother told me it wasn't *her* problem—he didn't give *her* any money—and it was his responsibility per the terms of their divorce to feed me. Call him, she told me; she didn't want to hear about it. And then she fucked off to Florida with my younger brothers to stay with her snowbird parents. And no, I was not invited.

That Christmas was miserable. The dorm was largely empty, as mostly everyone had gone home to see their folks or taken off on vacation. I spent a lot of time wandering around downtown Manhattan, trying to make my daily excursion to Mamoun's 75-Cent Falafel on Mac-Dougal Street take as long as possible.

The next year I took the leap and cut the cord, unceremoniously dropping out. I was, finally, *truly* on my own—a nineteen-year-old scrambling to make it and getting by with crappy jobs, while hustling for writing gigs, back when such a thing was possible.

Of course there were plenty of times in years to come when I was surviving on rice and beans and three-for-a-buck ramen noodles, and wondering how I was going to keep the lights on, but that was usually poverty of my own doing. At least now I was driving the car. Never again was I going to let the old man sandbag me. It was a tough lesson, but I caught on pretty quickly.

WHEN I WAS IN HIGH SCHOOL and was first accepted into the program, I was determined to become the best first-year film student ever. I had so many ideas. I was reading and writing all the time, plotting the films I was going to make and staying up to impossible hours to watch every old noir that came on *The Late, Late Show*, sneaking off to Greenwich Village art houses to see *Pink Flamingos* and Polanski's horror stuff, and even getting 16mm reels and one of those noisy old projectors from my local library to study up on Buñuel and Eisenstein and D. W. Griffith, not to mention Buster Keaton and Harold Lloyd. You have to remember this was the dark ages—before anyone even had VHS video players—and if you lived in suburbia and wanted to see anything that wasn't playing at the multiplex or the drive-in, you had to make a pretty big effort.

But when I finally landed at NYU, I let the situation suck the wind out of my sails. Truthfully, I did not really understand what it really took to make it back then. I was eighteen years old. I was just a puppy. College was supposed to be my ticket off the dismal planet my parents ruled, and now I was looking for an escape from this Promised Land that I had strived for so arduously. I started acting out. I was drinking too much, and smoking way more pot than I needed. I was behaving like an idiot, talking when I should have been listening.

But if the idea of college was to make friends and connections for the future, I was a booming success. I fell into an astonishing, wide net of musicians and artists, many of whom paved the way for adventure and love and heartbreak and hard-learned wisdom. Thirty years down the road, I'm still cavorting with many of them. But just as important, making friends who didn't come from my own air-conditioned slice of northeastern suburbia opened my eyes and showed me that there were plenty of people from fucked-up families crawling around lower Manhattan the same as I was, trying to find themselves. Maybe they weren't subjected to a never-ending cavalcade of verbal and emotional abuse, but I was definitely not alone.

We played in our punk rock and garage bands with battered equipment and drank beer on stoops in the East Village. We got drunk and listened to country music in dive bars. We crashed gallery openings to soak up the free wine. A big date was a tandoori special on East Sixth Street, with a bill of thirteen dollars, plus a forty-ouncer of cheap beer. After making a cheap record, my band somehow landed a record label and booking agent who sent us plane tickets to Berlin and Amsterdam and London. It was glorious.

A few years later, when I took another stab at finishing the four-year degree and went uptown to Columbia University, I was working full-time as the editor of a glossy professional wrestling magazine, *Main Event*. It was my first real job after leaving NYU. By then I was wearing some very smart-looking horn-rimmed glasses that I bought at Cohen's Fashion Optical® on Fourteenth Street, mostly because they were cheap and hard to break. A few years later they would become the apogee of hipster vogue, but at the time they were kind of stuck fashion-wise between "beatnik hangover" and "unrepentant nerd." Such is the way of the world.

When I applied to Columbia, the old man had assured me that "no way in hell are they going to let you into the Ivy League if you work for a *wrestling* magazine." He himself went to Brown and later MIT, and so spoke from a place of presumed and potent sagacity—but the brain trust at Columbia didn't it see it that way. *Main Event* may not have been *Vanity Fair*, but they obviously thought that a twenty-three-year-old running a high-circulation glossy newsstand magazine showed some sort of motivation and competence (I somehow forgot to mention my micro-career as porn novelist). Not only did they let me in, but they gave me a pass from their required "Columbia Method of Expository Writing" course. And I still got A's on all my papers. Go figure.

One semester later, despite having made the dean's list—at which point my mother demanded that I get her a Columbia bumper sticker for her car (I wisely demurred, since they are very difficult to remove, and of course Dad considered bumper stickers about as classy as vaginal warts)—I decided that I was not going to stick around to finish the degree. When I called to tell Dad, he told me good luck, and that if I needed anything, to be sure *not* to call him.

Decades later, he was still pissed off.

"You still blame me for your failure, don't you? You still think it was my fault that you dropped out of NYU," he railed. "You need to grow up already," he fumed.

Anytime in the last twenty or so years would have been a good time to discuss this, but he had never asked me why I decided to leave, or encouraged me to stay. And then of course I had the temerity to get accepted to a *better* school, only to drop out *again*.

Understandably, cutting short my tenure at Columbia was not a popular decision with either of my parents, but it was one that was actually measured and thoughtful, and one that I have never, not for a second, *ever* regretted.

I actually really liked going to Columbia, but another two and a half years seemed like a long time to dally in undergraduate school, and I had other wienies to roast. I went back to Europe with my band, and when I came back to New York, I got a better-paying magazine gig. Of course, it didn't matter.

"I can't believe they let you into Columbia . . . and then you dropped out!" he sputtered from behind the oxygen mask. I thought he might die on the spot. "You think you are smarter than the Ivy League?"

I must not be that smart, because even now I have no idea what that means. When I was a little kid, before the disappointment had set in, I heard a lot about how bright I was—an opinion largely based on my ability to fill in the little ovals on the old-school standardized tests with a fair amount of accuracy. I was always a little bit of a science geek, too—the space program made everyone nuts for slide rules and lab coats back then—and somehow this convinced him that I was going to grow up and become some sort of moneyed Superbrain.

Why not? When I was about eight, I built a computer. Actually it was just a kit from Edmund Scientifics®, this entirely awesome educational supply company that sold everything from Van de Graaff generators to ant farms to helium tanks—you name it. I bought a shiny, forty-foot weather balloon for only a few dollars, with aspirations to float it over by the high school and foment a suburban UFO scare. That dream is still alive.

The computer was plastic and had about five hundred separate parts. It was basically a very advanced adding machine that, when cobbled together, looked like a cross between a Frank Lloyd Wright ranch house and a lasagna, a fragile mess of sliding red and white plastic components and wire hinges. The readout was just three ones and zeros on cheap little plastic tumblers, but it taught some important lesson about Boolean logic and fundamental binary systems. A lot of the guys my age who built this thing when they were kids became wizards in the nascent programming industry. Obviously I did not.

One of the old man's favorite refrains was "You built a computer when you were eight, and then . . . nothing!"

Good grief, maybe they should just write that on my tombstone:

FORTY YEARS OF NOTHING.

Recently, I actually found one of those Edmund Scientifics kits online, selling for $100 (the original cost was

$8.99), and decided to try and build it again. I thought maybe it would give me some insight into who I was back then.

My father was right about one thing: I was very smart when I was eight.

7

PAPA JOE

n the hospital room in Arizona, while my father was simultaneously dying and dressing me down for being such an utter disappointment, I was thinking about a night when I was a freshman in college and he took me to dinner in Greenwich Village. After we ordered drinks he told me unceremoniously, "I wanted you to know that we buried your grandfather a few weeks ago." Then he called the waitress over and, after some small talk, ordered the veal.

I could barely figure out what that actually meant—*buried* him? What the fuck kind of euphemism was that? And why am I just hearing about this now? Oh, he was sick, and then he died. I am guessing there was a funeral, with a rabbi. And who sat *shiva*? This was a big deal. My father lived forty minutes away from me. He should have called me, but somehow he couldn't be bothered?

Now at dinner he tossed off the news of his father's death with such a lack of grace and humility that for the first time in my life I think I understood what *grace* and *humility* actually were, and found myself searching for a glimmer of them there in the void I was feeling while my father chatted up the waitress.

It was one of his worst habits, constantly interrupting dinner to bait service people into conversation: "Where do you go to school, dear? Oh, that's wonderful." Did he realize how condescending he sounded? I don't know why his wife didn't strangle him. And worse, unlike the suburbs and resorts where he lived and summered, waiters in fancy New York restaurants weren't college students. This was their real job, or they were actors or musicians hustling to make a living, in which case they fell into the same category under which he filed me—namely "Never Gonna Make It."

My relationship with my grandfather, whom we all called Papa Joe, was fairly simple. When I was a young child, he and my nana doted on me as best they could. He took me to Fenway Park and my very favorite place of all, the Boston Museum of Science, where I learned among other things about pendulums, photosynthesis, space travel, the internal combustion engine, and that in a vacuum, bricks and feathers fell at the same rate. They even had two towering airless plexiglass tubes in which they repeatedly dropped bricks and feathers to prove it. When I was eight, I could have watched that all day. Later, Nana took me to Howard Johnson® and watched me scarf down plate after plate of all-you-can-eat fried clams until I was practically shitting myself. I could not have asked for anything more.

They lived in an affluent Boston suburb in a giant house with an enormous out-of-tune grand piano that took up a mere postage stamp's worth of real estate in their football field of a living room. I think I was the only one who ever played it, clanging away with the perfect glee of a child let loose on such a contraption, harmony and melody be damned. At that age I was pure in my dedication to the avant and the atonal.

After Nana died—I was fourteen—Papa Joe seemed to deteriorate quickly. My father sold their house—the one he had grown up in—and after the funeral I had one last chance to scour it for artifacts before it all got tossed on the scrap heap. I came up with an antique humidor, which I later used to store my pot paraphernalia; my father's Flexible Flyer® sled, which I used to ride on the giant sloping hill out behind their house (one of the few times in my adolescence I can recall true bliss); and a beautiful edition of Edgar Allan Poe's *Tales of Mystery and Imagination* with gorgeous, tipped-in color plates by the great stained-glass artist and illustrator Harry Clarke. It is still the most beautiful book in my home.

And then my grandfather was in some sort of facility or another, where he lived with a woman, his contemporary, who was well enough taken care of to take care of him. I remember my father telling me the story of when Papa Joe had met her in the assisted-living home where he resided, and he had asked my father if he thought it was okay to kiss her before they moved into a room together. By that time, Papa Joe was well on his way to having lost all of his faculties to the dark murk of Alzheimer's, but that didn't stop my father from mocking him. *Oh look, Papa Joe is asking about sex, how cute!* He actually laughed out loud, and at that exact moment any doubts I had held about my father's lack of compassion and twisted sense of empathy evaporated perfectly. He was profoundly, almost elegantly, fucked.

I thought a lot about all the times we drove to Boston from our suburb in New Jersey to visit Nana and Papa Joe. My father never seemed happy to see his parents—they didn't have normal adult conversations or conversations at all, really. It was becoming increasingly clear my parents didn't really like each other, either. They fought on the car rides there and back. Invariably one of the kids would get carsick and puke somewhere along the Merritt

Parkway, which was somehow either his fault or hers, because why let an opportunity for a fight go by without leaping on it?

I recall several Passover seders and some Friday night dinners, back when they still lit the Shabbos candles, and Papa Joe would do the prayer over the wine (the whole thing, not the shortened version everyone knows). It was like "A Hard Rain's A-Gonna Fall" chanted in Hebrew in a dry Boston twang that fought a noble but losing battle against the guttural oomph of how *his* father must have delivered it every Friday night in his low-German accent. It was quite beautiful, a ray of antiquity shining through the gauzy New England ennui that hung like fog in their stuffy, formal dining room. But there was some darkness in it, too. Heavy times in Europe? I didn't know what exactly, though it was very real and spoke to a family history no one had ever talked about. My father looked at Papa Joe's prayer over the wine as some sort of parlor trick. *Look! Look at the Old Man do his act!* Papa Joe could have been an organ grinder's monkey. I knew the feeling well.

At dinner, after the epic *kiddush*, the grandparents never had anything to say to the kids. They suffered from the same inability to relate to youth that my parents did, and I could see their own disinterest in having fun emerge in stark relief: Unless there was a ball game, a science experiment, or a plate of fried clams to distract me, they were pretty much useless as company. And my folks were obviously miserable and unable to explain just what they were doing there together. Mostly they just glared at each other.

Later they started shipping me to Boston by plane, the old Eastern Air Lines® shuttle from Newark. It was a fast forty-five minutes on a cool jumbo jet, and they gave you plastic pilot's wings and a free can of ginger ale—heaven for an eight-year-old. I remember someone told me that Bobby Orr, the all-star defenseman for the Boston Bruins, was on my flight one time. I knew who he was—I used to go to the old Boston Garden with Papa Joe to see him play when I visited in winter—and I was excited to get an autograph, so I asked one of the flight attendants was it true, was it really Number 4, Bobby Orr? And if so, where was he? Meeting a celebrity athlete was wicked hot stuff for a little kid. "Oh, he's the one with all the blondes around him," I was told. And sure enough, there they were, buzzing like honeybees. It was the first time I had ever heard someone use a hair color as a gender assignment, and it was the first time I saw the power of fame close up. All of that potential sex was not lost on an eight-year-old boy, count on it.

I cherished all of those memories. And I instantly regretted that I had never made it my business to go see

Papa Joe again after that one time I had visited him years before, when he was newly situated in the nursing home, even if he didn't have a clue to who I was. But I was never encouraged or even asked to go, and at thirteen years old, that was just fine. The facility where he waited out his life smelled like oatmeal and death.

Still, when Papa Joe died, had I known, I would have climbed into whatever dress clothes I owned at the time, including the awful blue knit tie that I used to wear when I worked at Bamberger's° department store for a while in high school, and showed up to a funeral for a grand-father who was at the very least a part-time participant in my scant preteen happiness. I had good stories to tell about him taking me to the ballpark and the science museum, and the time I met Bobby Orr.

And that was the first time I thought about *my* father dying, right there at the Ponte Vecchio restaurant on Thompson Street, while my father flirted clumsily with the waitress. How would I feel about it when he was gone? Even then, I knew it wasn't going to be easy mourning for a guy who clearly didn't like me very much.

I DON'T KNOW HOW my father reacted to the news of *his* father's death or how he handled himself at the funeral.

Did he cry, or was it just business for him—an unpleasant obligation, a bit of family business that needed mopping up? I have no idea who was there or even where it was. And if he didn't tell me, who else didn't know? It was all very screwy and cold. He had enough aunts and uncles and cousins to fill a dozen P. G. Wodehouse novels. But after his mother died, I mysteriously never saw my father's extended family again.

I had spent wonderful days in Boston. I was made to feel these people were part of his life and would be part of mine, but it was all a lie. When I visited Boston as a kid, they would all come around and drink gin cocktails and ogle me, the precocious little kid who flew in from New Jersey to do magic tricks and tell jokes. Jewish boys are often like that. And then all of a sudden Nana died, and they were all gone. My father cut ties to family and friends easily—he was the least sentimental person I would ever know. But I didn't realize it then, and it was suddenly as if Boston itself had just fallen off the map.

I didn't go back until a dozen years later, when I had a gig with a porn magazine to do a story with an X-rated rock star who wanted to cruise the Combat Zone, which once upon a time was their sadly inadequate answer to Times Square. It was a great assignment, but what I really wanted to do was go over to the science museum and watch the feathers and bricks fall timelessly in those giant plexiglass tubes, then find a Howard Johnson and stuff my face with fried clams.

After the dinner with my dad, when he told me that he buried my grandfather, I walked a couple of blocks to Washington Square Park and cried and cried.

8

REQUIEM

After my very last moments with Dad in his Arizona hospital room, I left for New York. It didn't seem like the old man was in any immediate danger—after all, he had enough wind in his sails to blast me with his gale-force litany of disgust, now also known in family lore as the "You Suck Soliloquy." Unfortunately, that was about all he had.

When I arrived home I got the news that he had pitched his final inning and was being taken out of the game. He was in a coma. The next day they unplugged the machine, and he was gone. I prayed, as best I could, that he was in a better place. Anger in the afterlife seemed like the first condition for a haunting, and I wanted no part of that—I'd had enough of the earthly version. I didn't need any freaking phantasms coming around rattling chains or opening up my kitchen cabinets in the middle of the night just because I dropped out of college once or twice upon a time.

There would be no funeral, I was told—he had decided that funerals were ostentatious. He would be cremated, and there would be a "life ceremony," basically a posthumous banquet in his honor. Like a bar mitzvah, but without the crappy band.

I have to admit that I was fairly shocked by the decision. Cremation is strictly forbidden by Jewish law, and many Jews feel that to burn a body in an oven in the era after the Holocaust is also pretty tacky. It's a big party *don't.* Jews famously bury their dead quickly after death. "Life is for the living" is a very strong maxim in Judaism, which doesn't mean we don't mourn or carry the loving memories of the deceased in our hearts; it just means that traditionally we throw the fuckers in the ground, we say *kaddish,* we sit *shiva,* and we mourn, ritually and personally and profoundly, but there is a very high degree of closure and sense of moving on. There is no greater act of kindness than burying someone you love. And there is no such thing as a Jewish wake. Mostly, as a culture we just don't drink enough to make it worthwhile.

Frankly, I have no moral stake in this decision. Obviously everyone has the right to decide what happens to their bodies after they die. I have friends who believe in Eastern traditions of cremation and reincarnation, and I have agnostic friends who have given up on the church but want to hedge their bets on getting into heaven with proper Christian burials. I have one fabulously gay friend who has already put money away to hire several dozen professional mourners, all dressed like Jackie Kennedy. Actually, I think he has the right idea, and if he could get one of them to sob uncontrollably and hurl herself into the grave on top of the coffin and really make a scene, all the better. But who am I to judge? I might like to be blasted off into space—which, by the way, is still kosher. I checked. There are some loopholes that can be exploited, as long as the body is intact. After the *kaddish*, everyone could watch me take to the stars. And then sit *shiva* and eat a mountain of bagels and lox. I'm not without my ego, either.

When my father died there was no traditional, shared experience of grief, and no matter our relationship, I found that terribly sad. Who said *kaddish*? Also, I was raised and brought up in an emphatically Jewish household. I was told my whole life that this stuff matters, and then at the end of the day you break kayfabe and tell me it was all bullshit? I hate that kind of hypocrisy. It chafes. Then again, I saw how he dealt with the death of his own father, so I shouldn't possibly have had any expectations.

Ironically, I was the lucky one—I got my closure. The second he told me I was "a complete disappointment," we were done. Well, it did screw up my head for a long time after that, or else you and I wouldn't be here having this discussion. But at least I wasn't waiting around to say a prayer for him. His wife, though—and my brothers, whose experiences with the old man were wholly different from mine—didn't get that cold comfort. With this pending life-ceremony *megillah*, everything was held up in the air. And four years later, the ashes are *still* in her house, which I guess technically makes it a mausoleum.

It strikes me as a bit spooky, keeping the cremains around. I mean, it is a lovely home, but not a speck of dust has moved since his passing. All of his stuff still hangs in the living room, flawlessly announcing his highly curated version of good taste. It's as if he had constructed an air-conditioned crypt at the outskirts of the desert.

I'm not saying it's creepy or kooky like *Great Expectations*, or deluded like *Sunset Boulevard* or anything like that, but the fact that years later his voice is still on the outgoing voice-mail message on their house phone does strike me as somewhat ghoulish. I can imagine it must be traumatic to erase it, but imagine how people feel hearing it? When I want to call his wife to check in—and I do— I always call her cell phone. I can't handle the old man telling me to leave a message—or do *anything*, for that matter—from beyond the grave.

I think of Dad's widow often and hope she finds lots of love and light in her new life. I'm comforted to know she has her old friends and her *new* old friends—people whom my father had banished from their inner circle because he didn't tolerate people who liked to talk about their children—but how could anything replace the terrible void of losing her husband? They were married for thirty years and took amazingly good care of each other, walking in perfect lockstep, in an isolating and weird but loving co-dependency. Actually, she is much better away from him—easygoing, not quick to judge, genuinely interested in the lives of people around her—and she deserved to have the comfort of a traditional Jewish funeral. That's my feeling, anyway. (I have no doubt that later I will be told that I am wrong.) But given that my dad was a master of planning—he had every minute of his life worked out in advance; there were no audibles on the line of scrimmage for him, no going off-book, *ever*—and knowing, as we all do, that you don't get out of this world alive, the posthumous party-for-self seemed a hell of a lot like a calculated victory lap. *I don't want a funeral. I'm not that important. Instead we'll have this nice event, with canapés and a slide show.*

Golda Meir once said, "Don't be humble . . . you're not that great." But I have to hand it to him: For a guy who needed to let everyone know how awesome he was while appearing to be the Neoplatonic model of humility, it was a very good plan. The ultimate kayfabe.

* * *

THE DAY AFTER DAD DIED, I called his wife and offered to come out to Arizona right away and sit *shiva*. It felt like the right thing to do. At that point it wasn't about the dead; it was about the living. She told me not to come—it was too hot in Arizona in the summer—and just to wait until the life ceremony.

I wrestled with the decision for about ten minutes before deciding, with no further equivocating, that there was no way in hell that I was going to get up on a dais and talk about what a great guy my dad was.

My biggest conundrum at that point was telling his wife that I wasn't going to be joining them, in a way that expressed my very real sympathy for her but without coming right out and calling her dead husband a prick. Down the road we could talk—she wasn't an idiot; she knew we had our issues—but right then I owed her a note, at least.

I wrote that letter in my head every day for a week, over and over again. I started with a long version, explaining everything I ever felt about my dad. In my mind's eye, I could read all eight pages of the missive I had planned to write, as if it were a finished movie (I understand Hitchcock worked the same way). But then I decided it was way too much. For whom was I writing this: her or me? Maybe I should pick up the phone. And so I walked around the city for a couple of days thinking about how *that* conversation might go, and decided that it would open the doors to a long talk neither of us wanted to have. Anyway, I didn't really need to put her in a place where she would be forced to defend her dead husband.

Of course, I also spent the better part of two days trying to find the perfect stationery to write this letter on, because my usual motif of writing notes on the backs of old punk rock flyers was certainly not appropriate, and I had to find something that was warm—but neither happy nor maudlin—that would hold the ink of the old-fashioned fountain pen I intended to use to write the note. When one strives toward *menschdom*, details matter. Satisfied that I had found the correct, non-too-effete nature print silk-screened on thick eggshell vellum, $5.99 for one sheet with matching envelope at the local artisanal stationery shoppe, I chose an appropriate stamp (*never* metered postage for intimate correspondence) and composed a short note that was sturdy and unambiguous, telling her how deeply I felt her loss and how fortunate my dad was to have her, and that it was with great regret that I would not be there for the life ceremony, such as it was. No explanation was offered, because after everything, I realized none was needed.

9

PUNCHING BACK

Now I am going tell you something I have never told anyone before. It's still very difficult for me to talk about. I didn't even tell Dr. Headshrinker, not until after I wrote this and sent it to her.

When I was in junior high, I was bullied by a boy much bigger and stronger than me. One day he beat me up and took my green army field jacket I had saved up for and bought at an army surplus store on Route 1. It probably doesn't seem like a big deal now—teenagers seem to always have those jackets—but in 1978 you couldn't just go to the mall and buy rebel couture. I lived in a sea of Sears Toughskins®, and I had sought it out very specifically because I saw John Lennon wearing one in a photo. In my pre-punk, proto-hippie daze, he was my authority-questioning, anti-establishment hero. No one else I knew had anything nearly as cool.

With my long hair and mirrored aviator shades, I thought I looked pretty badass in that jacket, but back then I was anything but, and a few blows to the head later—in broad daylight, as they say, right on the fucking sidewalk when I was walking home from school—it was his. He rained fists on my face and took the jacket right off my back as cars filled with kids and parents drove by on their way to after-school piano lessons and gymnastics.

When I was in junior high, the kids who shared my interest in smoking pot were not mellow stoners—they were animals. Getting high with them was like climbing into a lion's cage. They were unpredictable, and had little higher calling than to get fucked up. They championed Lynyrd Skynyrd (the band most overrated by morons and most underrated by Stones fans, who should know better), and mediocre, second-tier hard-rock acts like Mahogany Rush (who were basically a Jimi Hendrix cover band with a bigger phase-shifter). They were blunt-edged-and-dangerous New Jersey rednecks.

The only reason I ever hung out with them was because they knew where to score pot, or they sold it themselves. Also pills, lots of pills. I used to buy black beauties and bust them open and snort the amphetamine sulfate powder on the inside, which, if I had been a real beatnik—"burning for the ancient heavenly connection to the starry dynamo in the machinery of night" or some such nonsense—might have been a very hip thing to do. But at thirteen years old, out behind the VFW hall around the corner from my junior high school at eight in the morning, not so much. I was pretty miserable at home, so this was how I got my kicks.

Eventually I came in from the cold—the pot thing evened itself out and I fell in with some dilettante Dead Heads and guys who liked to jam on Black Sabbath— great stuff for your budding drummer. They were actually decent musicians—guys I'd later form bands with to play keg parties and street fairs, which mostly kept me out of trouble (idle hands and all that). The weed became a catalyst for creativity and not the activity itself, exactly as it should have been. But for now, I had to take it where I found it.

The boy who beat me up spent his weekends drinking beer and lifting weights with his father. I think he could bench-press over three hundred pounds, which is just monstrous for a fourteen-year-old. He could have taken my head off like the twist-cap on a bottle of Budweiser®. I saw his garage once when I went over there to buy some weed, and it could not possibly have been more different from our garage, which was so clean it could have doubled as an art gallery. Our snow shovel, practically floating on its proprietary hook, was like a Duchamp masterpiece. My basketball, which also had its own very specific place where it *had* to be returned after we played HORSE in the driveway, could have been an early Koons installation. This kid's garage, aside from the beer cans that littered the place, looked exactly like what I imagined a medium-security penitentiary would, with free weights and barbells everywhere, the merest ode to joy coming from a *Hustler* centerfold taped haphazardly to the wall. Ashtrays were filled to overflowing. I have to admit, though, that I was kind of in awe that he was allowed to drink and smoke with his dad, even if it was only on weekends.

Getting beaten up and ripped off right out in the open was pretty much the worst ten minutes of a three-year junior high school career that was almost 100 percent miserable.

What hurt the worst is that I couldn't fight back—the son of a bitch was not only a thousand times stronger than me but also full of fierce, unchecked aggression that just came naturally to him, like walking or breathing. He could fight without even thinking about it. The next day he came to school wearing my jacket, and I had to suck it up and take it like a giant fucking pussy. I was far too embarrassed and ashamed to tell anyone about it, and whenever anyone asked me where my cool army jacket was, I just tried to disappear.

If you've never been beaten up, here's something you should know: It usually doesn't hurt as much as you might think it would. Everybody should have their asses kicked at least once. It builds character. It teaches you not to be afraid of getting hit.

You get punched in the head and the gut and then you get up and walk home and try not to cry, because it is a very lonely feeling. Maybe if you got socked in the eye, you go get a bag of ice or frozen peas or a steak to stop the swelling. You'll probably be sore as hell, but after a few days you'll be fine. Except for the humiliation. That could take a while.

I spent weeks brooding on it, wondering what I should do. I thought maybe I'd bring my Swiss Army knife to school, and the next time he started pushing me around I'd cut him. Then I realized that the knife was actually less threatening and more pathetic than I was—its biggest features were a toothpick and tweezers. So I did my best to avoid him, but he still went out of his way to catch me walking home. He got off on scaring the shit out of me. Just watching me flinch made him howl in glee.

Only recently have I even allowed myself to think about this—it really is just about the worst memory of my entire childhood, and it went on for the better part of seventh grade. But I'm glad I did. When I finally got up the nerve to look up this boy who made my life so miserable, I found him on a social media site sporting a ribbed wifebeater and clutching the saddest-looking shih tzu I had ever seen. I felt sorry for him—the shih tzu, that is. It's terrible, I know, but thirty-five years later, seeing him looking so pathetic made me feel just a little bit better.

MY FATHER WENT TO a very elite prep school and knew well the value of the pedigree, if not the actual education. He graduated high school in a class of just eighteen kids, and all of them went on to Ivy League universities. It's also probably worth mentioning that the town that he grew up in was largely considered one of the best school districts in the entire *country*, and even *that* wasn't good enough for his parents.

My junior high school was like a work camp for children, and that's no joke. They weren't teaching much over there other than conformity and supplication. Show up on time, follow the rules, and get out in one piece. Punch the clock. Do not talk back. It wasn't education— it was crowd control.

The school district we lived in was largely made up of working-class Protestants and Catholics—third-generation Americans like me, but whose grandparents or great-grandparents came from a much different Europe than did mine. The usual stereotypes often prevailed, and there was a low-spoken but palpable strain of anti-Semitism.

There was also a bar directly across the street from my junior high (who zoned these things, W. C. Fields?) where the guards—that is to say, the teachers—drank after work. They also sold beer and liquor ("packaged goods," as they're called in New Jersey), and I bought a six-pack there once when I was still underage (no one ever gave a second look at even the most horrendously fake IDs they used to sell in Times Square for five bucks). The place felt like the Azkaban prison in the Harry Potter books. It was truly soul-sucking—just being in there for a few minutes made me feel like I would never, ever be capable of another cheerful thought.

My mother wanted to send me to a private school, but my father would have no part of that. "He told me, 'No, I'm not spending the money on him,' and that was the entire conversation. I knew that the school you were going to wasn't good enough. You were bored and starting to get in trouble. We certainly could have afforded it, but he was already past caring. He gave up on you the second he realized that you were not going to be a tennis-playing preppy like he was. He was done with you, and just moved on to your brothers."

I asked her how old I was when that happened.

"Nine," she told me flatly. She carried that sadness with her for a long time.

MY FATHER MADE IT A BIG POINT to distance himself from his own privileged upbringing, and yet, the summer when I turned nine, I was shipped off to the same twee and very expensive sailing camp on Cape Cod where he went when he was a kid. I was supposed to come out the other end *transformed*. Not quite like in the movie *Tommy*, when the little boy's dad takes him to a brothel to visit Tina Turner as the Acid Queen, but you get the idea.

At camp I was lonely and miserable. I had zero in common with those kids, and I didn't want to go sailing. All I wanted to do was play baseball. And I was the only Jewish boy there. The moment the other kids figured that out, I got a lot of strange looks. Many of them had never seen one before. At least one kid felt my head to see if I had horns.

The camp was predominantly old-school Boston Catholic. They said the Lord's Prayer as a large group before Sunday breakfast. I had no idea what it was all about, except it was some sort of honor for a boy to be chosen to begin the prayer for the entire group, and for some reason no one ever picked me.

The old man thought these were the people I should be making friends with. I guess he hoped some old-fashioned New England gentility was going to rub off on me, but it was never going to happen. We just vibrated at different frequencies.

Looking back, I can see pretty clearly that the moment I got back from camp and he realized that I had not been transmogrified into a miniature version of himself is the *exact* moment my mother was talking about. *Quod erat demonstrandum*, I was a failed project. "There were two more children coming down the pipeline," my mom told me. "He thought maybe he'd have better luck with them."

THE KID I PUNCHED was my size, and it was a fair fight. That's my story and I am sticking to it. I balled up my fist and wound up like a cartoon character. Or perhaps Greg "The Hammer" Valentine, who was one of my favorite wrestlers in those days. He was pretty cartoonish, actually, with giant forearms totally out of proportion to his body, which made him look like Popeye with cheap peroxide hair. But there was nothing fake about the way I hit the kid, right on the buzzer. He went flying backward over a lunch table, ass-over-teakettle as they say, and he landed in a heap. I wish I could have hit the bully like that. Given a fair fight, apparently I had some tooth, and I'd be lying if I said it didn't feel good.

His crime was calling me "hymie" and a "fucking kike." I don't remember how the argument started—some lunchtime bullshit between hormone-crazed thirteen-year-olds—but it was probably as much my fault as anyone's. Between worrying about being beaten up every day after school and dreading getting screamed at by my mom about what a deadbeat my dad was (never mind Dad's constant put-downs and willful neglect), I was probably just wanting for some attention. But when I punched that boy, it was *righteous*. He had crossed the line. "Asshole," "douchebag," or "dickwad," I could walk away from. "Hymie" and "kike," not so much. So I hit him.

I didn't tell my folks when I got beaten up, and I certainly wouldn't have told my parents about this, either. But seeing as I was picked up by the scruff of my neck by the Frankenstein-like shop teacher on lunch duty that day, and shuttled straight down to the vice principal's office—my feet didn't touch the floor even once—I really didn't have much of a say in the matter.

I was sentenced without trial to a three-day suspension. Oddly, the vice principal, a beleaguered forty-year-old man with acne scars and a tired pompadour, didn't have anything to say about the Jew slur. I guess he didn't consider it any worse than the shit kids usually say in cafeteria fights, of which there were plenty. Every day someone else got creamed.

I had been taught emphatically in bar mitzvah classes that this sort of thing should never go unremarked— that this is exactly how a lot of bad shit gets started—and I mistakenly thought he would see the purity of my cause. I was wrong, of course. My parents didn't come around to my way of thinking, either.

What the hell? Don't I get some respect for standing up for myself and dropping that anti-Semitic fuck? I owned it like a six-pointed blue badge of courage. Jews were an abject minority in that school, and the vice principal probably thought we were a bunch of whiners (which may or may not have been true), but couldn't he at least *pretend* to be concerned?

We all knew how this was supposed to play: My mother was supposed to be upset because her kid got into a fight and was suspended. And my father was supposed to tell me sternly that I should have been the bigger man and walked away, while telling me out of the side of his mouth how proud he was that I stood up for myself and clobbered this Hitler youth. Well, that didn't happen. My father just told me that he was very disappointed in me and then let my mother deal with it. Not surprisingly, she chose to make the whole episode all about *her*, screaming at me like a lunatic, "I can't believe I have the kind of son who gets into fights! What did I ever do to deserve this?"

Whatever happened to good old-fashioned Jew paranoia? And getting on the phone to the Jewish Defense League or the junior high school principal or whoever's job it should have been to get to the bottom of this scurrilous rash? She spent most of her free time in those days on some vague Jewish charity—from the outside, it would seem that she'd be down with the cause and take this shit to heart—but it was all kayfabe crap, just something to do with the ladies. No one had ever threatened her for being Jewish. Her biggest problem related to her Jewish-ness was opening the package of the kosher turkey breast every Wednesday, which, admittedly, was no little feat—the tinfoil tray it came in could *cut* you.

What did my parents know, anyway? It's not like they ever stood up for anything in their lives. They were suburban nihilists—they believed in nothing!

Except, of course, that teachers were to be obeyed and *never* questioned—and let me tell you, there were some rotten ones in that school who deserved some serious scrutiny. They were overworked, bitter, untalented, likely hungover from drinking at the bar across the street, and existentially crushed by their shitty jobs.

I had teachers who would lament wistfully, "These are the best days of your life. Cherish them—you'll wish you could relive them." Really? Now, *that* was heartbreaking, that an actual adult would look back with fawning nostalgia to a time when they lived with their parents, had no money, and never got laid. Boy oh boy, their lives must have sucked! And these were the people to whom I was supposed to pay blind obeisance?

And then there was the lunatic fringe, represented by my English teacher, who wanted to ban *Slaughterhouse-Five* and *Catcher in the Rye* from the school library—the former because it questioned the existence of God; the latter because it promoted anti-social behavior. I'm not sure what it says about me, but as you now know, I believe in both of those things.

Parent-teacher conferences were the worst. Even when I was in grade school and was getting straight A's, my father would go to these things with the same seriousness of purpose that Churchill brought to Malta, and he would inevitably return with the report that I was not applying myself. I had heard rumors that when some kids brought home good grades, their parents rewarded them. Me—I got yelled at, because I somehow hadn't managed to build an atom smasher and win the science fair. I built that computer and then . . . NOTHING!!!! I could never catch a break.

Also, apparently I had an attitude problem.

I'm not quite sure where I learned not to trust authority figures, although it certainly had something to do with my friend Eric's dad's record collection. Listening to George Carlin and Bob Dylan definitely set me on the path. Whatever mentoring my old man gave me was worse than useless—it was *neutering*. He had impressed upon me for so long that there was only one way of being a success in life, but I was just never any good at kissing ass.

"Your father was successful because he was very good at sucking up and selling the message that the people in authority needed to deliver," one of his former colleagues told me. "That's how it was done in his world, that's how he got ahead. And that's why he resented you, because at an early age you had this great sense of self. You weren't afraid to say 'fuck you,' and this sort of independence was threatening to him. He took it very personally— if you were to ever become a success, it meant that his system was flawed."

What my father never understood is that I never wanted to be a rebel—at least not one without a cause. James Dean tried that, and look where it got him. And that whole Marlon Brando thing in *The Wild One*: "What are you rebelling against?" "I dunno, whatta ya got?"—it was sexy as hell, but it never struck me as being all that bright. It was kind of like screaming at the rain. Fighting with everyone seemed a very unhappy road to travel. Call me a hippie, I don't care: I am quite certain that life is best when it is an expression of love. But know this, too: After I slugged that kid in the cafeteria, no one ever called me "hymie" again.

WRITING THIS NOW, I'm thinking maybe it's about time I found some compassion for that bully. Actually, there was a real loneliness about that photo. That dog of his wasn't exactly the kind of pet a tough guy keeps, and the way he was clutching it just made him look desperate for some love. Maybe drinking beer and pumping iron in the shadow of a *Hustler* centerfold wasn't the nurturing environment he needed to blossom into a fully functional adult human being. Maybe he just wasn't equipped to liberate himself from a cycle of violence and stupidity. Of course, maybe he was just a dick, and still is. Who knows? I'm not going to call the dude—he probably doesn't even remember me. Beating me out of my jacket was just another day at the office for him.

When I started writing this part of the story, I felt sick to my gut. The memory was so visceral and so dizzyingly ugly that it made me queasy, as if I were actually being punched in the stomach all over again. Telling the world about it, though, has finally put me in the position of power. Finding compassion and forgiveness for this ape meant I had the potency to grant long-distance clemency—like I was the governor of some far-off, touchy-feely utopia, where feelings were the coin of the realm. It didn't suck. As it turns out, it was the best way to show some mercy on myself.

After I sent Dr. Headshrinker the story I wrote about being bullied and confessed that I still feel haunted by the entire experience, she asked me, "Mike, why do you keep punishing yourself for something someone did to you when you were a kid? Holding on to this is just a way of beating yourself up. Forgiveness is about accepting that you no longer want to hold on to anger, that you are ready to let go, that you no longer want to live clouded by pain. Forgiveness is how you separate yourself from all of this hurt and resentment. Wasn't it bad enough the first time?"

As always, she has a nice way of being sympathetic while also cutting through the bullshit. And so, there it is—*Et ego te absolvo a peccatis tuis . . . poof!*—and like magic, I feel a whole lot better. I've moved on. I may have been the victim of a bully, but I'm not defined by it. I know it's hackneyed, but we don't measure ourselves by how often we get knocked down; we measure ourselves by how quickly we get up.

But absolution for a boy who was mean to another boy is far easier to accept and deliver than the same indulgence for my father—an adult who was mean to a child. Perhaps there are some things that are just not forgivable? Still, as Dr. Headshrinker astutely pointed out, the pardon is not intended for *my father*—after all, he's gone—but as a gift of compassion that I give to *myself.* I just wish it were that easy. It took me thirty-five years to be able to confront one shitty afternoon in junior high school, so maybe I'm not quite the champ I like to think I am.

10

(TALKIN' 'BOUT) MY GGGGENERATION

The day before I was born—August 2, 1964— Jack Warner shut down the Warner Bros.® cartoon division, sending Bugs Bunny, Porky Pig, and Daffy Duck off to find a new home. A few days later, two American warships were attacked in the Gulf of Tonkin, leading to the eponymous resolution and the official beginning of the Vietnam War.

Earlier that year, the Beatles appeared on *The Ed Sullivan Show*. My parents watched it, but it didn't mean anything to them. None of it did. The Vietnam War didn't even get a reaction from them: Years later, my mom told me they never discussed it, which I find odd if not palpably distressing.

When I was born, Dad was twenty-seven. Mom was twenty-four. They were part of a wave known as the Silent Generation, largely thanks to a 1951 *Time* magazine cover story that asked the question, "Is it possible to paint a portrait of an entire generation?" And then it did, more or less, exactly that, describing "a remarkably clear area of agreement on the state of the nation's youth."

If you were to believe everything in the story, people born between 1925 and 1942—namely, my folks—did not question authority. They believed in order and the status quo. They were not a generation strong on leadership, and eventually they became famous as the only generation never to produce an American president. Their worldview seemed to be mostly concerned with their own well-being, "working fairly hard and saying almost nothing. The most startling fact about the younger generation is its silence . . . today's younger generation is a still, small flame. It does not issue manifestoes, make speeches or carry posters." Incidentally, they were also the last generation to grow up without television.

My father graduated from high school in 1955 and shipped off to the Ivy League, believing that the nascent rock 'n' roll music was teeny-bopper nonsense and well beneath him. My mom graduated in 1957 and danced to Chuck Berry and Fats Domino at her prom. They were both just a little bit too old, but definitely too square and too neurotic, to have enjoyed any of the classically transcendent 1960s experiences. Unlike my dad, however, my mom got to discover at least for a few moments that it was okay to be a teenager. The year she graduated high school was pretty much the first time in America when it was actually cooler to be young than old. She kept a little bit of that spirit intact until it was drummed out of her by my old man. It would become his goal to cure us all of our youth.

Dad graduated Brown University in 1959 and was sprung from grad school, the very prestigious MIT Sloan School of Management, in 1961. Mom graduated college the same year from Lesley University, a smallish school in Cambridge, Massachusetts, where MIT was also located.

I once asked my mom about what drew her to my dad. Surely she must have been in love with him at some point? They got married and had three kids, after all. She had no good answer except that "he came from Boston and went to Brown, and his mother dressed him in Brooks Brothers. He seemed very nice." He also played tennis, which she loved, and he took her to see the Boston Pops, which had impressed her. It was the ultimate middlebrow reach for upper-class sophistication—the Gucci bag of dating. During the years they went to see the orchestra, the program hardly changed: It was all Gershwin, all the time—the perfectly modern soundtrack for kayfabe romance.

My parents were married in a hurry, sailing straight-away into the greatest uninterrupted period of economic expansion in American history. Their timing was great: If you graduated college in the late 1950s or early 1960s, you could make some real coin—unemployment was at 1 percent. Inflation was practically unheard of. Houses were affordable. Cities bustled with jobs, and the great suburban dream was alive.

This was the stage on which my father chose to create his perfect life. He would prosper in real estate. Mom would learn her station in life as an elementary school teacher. It was all she ever wanted—suburban bliss wrapped in the idyll of Formica® prosperity and wall-to-wall carpet. Bouncing babies who would grow up to be nice Jewish boys or girls and give her plenty of nice Jewish grandchildren. She would have lots of friends who talked a lot about nothing. Her world was a small one.

For him, though, it was hardly enough. Or maybe too damn much. He once told me that he would have been very happy not having any kids. Of course, he dialed that back the very second he said it—he didn't *regret* having children—but the message was clear. He had little room for anyone or anything that didn't serve his ego.

My father grew up in a gorgeous New England home, surrounded by a stone wall that was probably built by Robert Frost, but he was determined to move my mom into a house well below their means. By contrast, Mom had grown up in relative poverty. Her parents were the children of poor immigrants who spoke Yiddish in the home, and when they went to the synagogue, they usually called it going to *shul*, a term that my father disdained. "*We* don't go to *shul*. *We* go to *temple*," he corrected me, and with far more anger in his voice than should ever have been indicated. It took me years to figure out why that was, exactly—didn't suburban Jews have enough problems without having to kayfabe where they went to worship? But *shul* was old-school Yiddish, and Yiddish was *low*. It was *ethnic*, and not the kind of monkey-talk that hyper-assimilated society Jews in Boston liked to bandy about.

When my parents were ready to buy the house in which they would raise their family (we lived in a tiny apartment until I was four, when my twin brothers were born), my mother lobbied hard for a home that she absolutely loved, just across the town line in a terrific school district, with lots of trees and nice families. She was shut down by my father who insisted they buy an innocuous split-level in a cookie-cutter, post-Levittown development just a few blocks away.

The difference in prices of the two houses was nominal—two thousand dollars, Mom told me years later. She adored the home she had chosen, and knew it would be better for the kids. But as was his wont, he used his checkbook to oppress her and stay in control. He always seemed be trying to teach her some sort of tough-love lesson, but usually it just came across as mean.

"That," she later told me, "is when I first realized that we weren't in this together. We weren't friends, and I couldn't be in love with someone who wasn't even my friend. And I just had twins. We had three kids—there was no way I could leave. In those days you didn't really have a choice. I was stuck."

MY GENERAL SENSE IS THAT it is a little too breezy to paint entire generations with one broad stroke. The so-called Silent Generation that produced my parents also produced Gloria Steinem, Andy Warhol, Little Richard, Martin Luther King Jr., Abbie Hoffman, and Bob Dylan, to name but a few, but those people became my heroes, not theirs.

According to the kind of pop sociology that loves to put everything in boxes, twenty years or so make up a generational era: The Baby Boomers (1946 to 1964 or so) followed the Silent Generation, which was followed by the so-called Generation X (roughly 1964 to the early 1980s, depending on who you ask), who grew into an era sadly characterized by Wall Street greed, the dismantling of the middle class, and a return to Eisenhower-era anti-intellectualism, largely stewarded by Ronald Reagan and his dingbat "Just-Say-No" wife, Nancy.

"There are times . . ." Hunter Thompson mused, "when even being right feels wrong. What do you say, for instance, about a generation that has been taught that rain is poison and sex is death? If making love might be fatal and if a cool spring breeze on any summer afternoon can turn a crystal blue lake into a puddle of black poison right in front of your eyes, there is not much left except TV and relentless masturbation. It's a strange world. Some people get rich and others eat shit and die."

Right now we're looking at a bumper crop of Millennials (early 1980s to the early 2000s) coming of age in a culture moving so fast that it seems nearly impossible to gain purchase on anything, what with life whipping by on tiny screens, a free fall of highly disposable ones and zeros. Presumably this generation or their spawn are the ones that are going to inherit the Earth. I guess we'll just have to see what's left for them in another forty years.

By the loosest definition, I am sitting in the very last row on the Baby Boomer bus, but I wholeheartedly reject being any part of that group. Bill Clinton, the very epitome of the Baby Boomer, was born in 1946, and clearly I am not from his generation. But neither am I part of the next broadly defined group, Generation X.

People born in 1964 or so share a unique historical catbird seat. We've benefited directly from the counter-culture and music of the 1960s, and a heavy dose of the jaded cynicism and awesome bombast of the 1970s, but we're still young enough to have embraced first-wave punk rock, become self-aware through the Reagan years, and grown into the Internet without being formed by it. I was old enough to see Jethro Tull when they were still a hot ticket. I remember where I was when Elvis died *and* the first time I heard Grandmaster Flash, Run-DMC, and Public Enemy.

When *Never Mind the Bollocks, Here's the Sex Pistols* came out in 1977, I was thirteen years old, and the TV news was screaming about this fresh threat to youth: *Punk Rock: Violence, Anarchy, and Chaos! Film at 11!* I happened into a record store where a couple of stoned hippies had a copy up by the cash register. I immediately wanted to buy it, and the first one told me, "Just take it. Play it for your friends," and the second one chortled, "And then you won't have any friends!" They may have high-fived each other. They were ridiculously pleased with themselves.

I brought it home and played it for my pal Eric, and it totally blew us away. It was just so *big* and *angry*—the logical extension of Bob Dylan's rage against the machine distilled into pure, astringent snarl. *How does it feeeeeeeel??? Pretty vaaaaaaaaaaaaaaacaant.* Ironically, there was more genuine anarchy in Dylan's lyrics than in the Sex Pistols'. He had taught us—contrary to what our parents believed—that not everything had to make sense. But that was an old revolution; this one was ours. Our personal *Ubu Roi*.

We sat in my bedroom and quite literally watched the record go around and around on the record player, amazed at the *new* sound of rebellion unlocking itself from the spinning plastic disk and pumping ferociously out of my old speakers with the tidal force of Noah's flood. The impact was inescapable: Ten years later, I was in my own punk rock band, touring England and opening up for the Ramones.

My parents were never interested in making waves. They were very much those people buttonholed in the *Time* magazine story. "There is also the feeling," the article went on, "that it is neither desirable nor practical to do things that are different from what the next fellow is doing."

Let's face it: It's a square world. America, a country built on rugged individualism, still puts a high premium on "fitting in." Growing up, I was told that there were rules that *had* to be followed and that I must *always* obey my parents, teachers, and future employers—*all* adults, really. That's what they had been taught, and now they were carrying the freight. But there was a palpable sense that my parents, and everyone of their generation—at least the ones who *seemed* to be in charge—were completely full of shit.

When I was a little kid, the Vietnam War was on television every night. It was on the front page of the paper, which I looked at every day (mostly just to read *Peanuts*), but there it was—a big ugly war, and inevitably a photo of our dour, unctuous president, Richard Nixon, lying about one thing or another. Thousands of young men died, and for some reason we never knew any of them. It didn't touch our lives directly, and so it was as if it weren't even happening. It was surreal. And when I asked questions about it, I got no good answers. Not that I needed a treatise on the Gulf of Tonkin or My Lai or the invasion of Cambodia, but no one had the patience to talk to me about *any* of it, and it just made me trust adults less and less. I never got a decent explanation for *anything.* Everything just *was.*

I remember lining up for gas during the so-called Energy Crisis in 1973. You could only buy gasoline on certain days, depending on your license plate number. Later, of course, I found out that it was all bullshit, there was no real oil shortage—it was just some giant reindeer game being played by a bunch of dudes who looked like they should have been the heels on *Florida Championship Wrestling.* Perhaps indicative of nothing, 1973 was also the year the designated hitter was introduced in baseball—a signal shift of nuance to power in the national pastime.

The next year I watched the president of the United States resign on live television for crimes far too complex for a ten-year-old to ever fathom, only to be given a "Get Out of Jail Free" card by the guy that replaced him. You didn't have to be a poli-sci major (let alone an adult) to know that there was something seriously stinky about the way the world was being run.

Remember how nuclear power and the metric system were going to save us? And then in 1979, Three Mile Island happened. It was the worst nuclear accident in American history. They made a film about it called *The China Syndrome*, referring to the fanciful idea that if Three Mile Island had been a *full* nuclear meltdown, the core would have burned completely through the Earth, from Pennsylvania straight down to Shanghai. That didn't *quite* happen, but you had to know you were fucked pretty goddam good when they got a couple of lefties like Jane Fonda and Jack Lemmon to star in a movie about the failure of your industry.

Soon after that I went to see the *No Nukes* concert movie, which you probably don't remember. It was a nice moment—the last optimistic gasp of a superannuated protest movement—but a year later, no one seemed to care. Jimmy Carter put up solar panels on the White House in 1976, and Ronald Reagan tore them down in 1980. Reagan's swagger was a clear sign that the jocks had made a comeback after America had lost its way in the 1960s and '70s. It was time to vanquish the hippie scourge once and for all.

ACTUALLY, WHEN REAGAN CAME IN, the new and very real scare wasn't nuclear *power*, but rather nuclear *arms*. The Cold War had been rebooted: USA vs. Russia! Good vs. Evil! It was just like wrestling, except it was *real*. And yet no adult that I knew growing up ever seemed to worry about nuclear power *or* the arms race. Maybe they found Reagan's foreign policy shift from the old doctrine of "mutually assured destruction" to the rosier vision of "a winnable nuclear war" to be some sort of balm. I have no idea, because all my parents and teachers ever seemed to worry about was *drugs*.

How many completely insane drug scare stories did I have to weather before I was certain that they were either lying and/or had zero clue as to what they were talking about? Either way, with every idiotic story that was meant to "scare me straight," all they did was prove that nothing that came out of their mouths could be trusted.

"Did you hear about the babysitter who was on drugs? When the parents called home to see how their child was, she said, 'The baby? He's almost done!' Thankfully the parents raced home to save their child—the babysitter was so stoned she thought the infant was a turkey, and tried to roast him in the oven! That's what drugs do to you."

I heard that story so many times, usually introduced with the old chestnut, "This happened to someone a friend of mine knew in California"—the signature riff of the urban myth. Did they really believe this crap? I still think about it: Just what kind of fabulous drugs does one have to take to mistake an infant for a turkey? And even if you are that stoned, is your reaction really going to be to ignore a baby's protests as you baste it with butter and paprika?

It remains one of my favorite jewels of the entire drug-scare-story genre, although honorable mention must be given to the pantheon of cautions involving people who smoked pot and then leapt enthusiastically to their deaths off of tall buildings, believing they could fly. To listen to my parents and teachers, kids were just *sailing* off rooftops. It was as if you could hardly walk down the street without the risk of being flattened by a plummeting pot smoker.

The films we watched in health class were classics of the scare genre: Smoking weed led to heroin addiction and death, usually swinging at the end of a rope in a jail cell. Marijuana turned you into a homosexual, a murderer, or at the very least, a terminally unemployed waste product bound for a desolate existence on skid row, wherever that was. Women who smoked pot were of loose moral character and to be *shunned*. Men who smoked pot grew *breasts*. For anyone with half a brain, this was obviously the biggest load of bullshit ever foisted upon America's youth—so ridiculous that eventually my friends and I began borrowing these films from the library to watch *while* we got stoned.

But such was the timbre of the day. When I was fifteen and got caught smoking weed, my mother's reaction was, "I should send you away." Seriously. Her words. *I should send you away.* Who says that? My father, on the other hand, generally solved these sorts of problems by ignoring them. Not caring made everything so much easier. All of that being said, I would be lying to you if I said I wouldn't be pretty freaking upset if I caught my teenager getting high. Then again, I wouldn't be shipping them off to reform school if I did. My instinct would be to tell them the truth.

Of course, times have changed. A couple of months ago I was driving in the car with my mom and Brother No. 1, the Wall Street *macher*, and Mom asked him, "I hear there is money in marijuana. Is there a marijuana stock I should invest in?"

Naturally, mellow hippie that I am, I blew my top. "You are really going to ask Goldman Sachs over here how you can make money on the marijuana market? Really?? Am I the only one here who sees the irony in this? Do I really have to point out just what kind of hypocrite this makes you? You were going to 'send me away,' and now—just because all of a sudden you think there is some money in it—you think it is okay to basically become a pot dealer????"

As you can imagine, this line of patter got me exactly nowhere. "Shut up, Michael. I don't want to hear your shit," she told me, not really twigging to the irony after all, and that was that for the moment. I understand she asked him about the pot stocks again later, before deciding to hang on to her Exxon® and Monsanto® preferred.

MY OLD MAN MAY HAVE GIVEN UP on me in 1973—the year I turned nine—but that was also the year of my grand awakening. Never mind the energy crisis or the designated hitter; 1973 was one of the greatest years for pop music, ever. The radio was a vessel for genius, and New York's finest Top 40 radio station, WABC, formed me.

That year, Stevie Wonder had two of his heaviest Clavinet numbers, "Superstition" and "Higher Ground" ("Master Blaster" and "You Haven't Done Nothin'" being the others); Al Green had "Here I Am (Come and Take Me)"; Curtis Mayfield was doing "Superfly"; the O'Jays had a number one with "Love Train"; Sly Stone was still a force with "If You Want Me to Stay"; Marvin Gaye shot way above my nine-year-old head with "Let's Get It On"; and the Temptations ended their psychedelic era with the epic, truly harrowing "Papa Was a Rolling Stone," which plainly scared the shit out of me. Every one of those songs was like a bolt of lightning.

Of course there was also a mega-ton of crud like Gilbert O'Sullivan and Tony Orlando that year. There would always be crappy pop music—name the year, and you can easily find something that will make you want to crawl into a hole. But this was also the year of Bobby Pickett and the Crypt Kickers' "Monster Mash," a confection so perfectly concocted it would have been a hit no matter when it dropped, and Diana Ross's "Touch Me in the Morning," the topic of which even now torches the imagination.

Mostly I listened on my little clock radio that I had covered in stickers, including a couple of Wacky Packages® ("Vile" soap and "Crust" toothpaste) and one of those stupid labels that people put on their lapels at trade shows that say HELLO, MY NAME IS. I wrote MIKE'S RADIO on it in multicolored balloon letters, the hepcat font for nine-year-olds, as seen in *Dynamite* magazine. The clock radio had been a present from my parents, presumably to help me wake up and get to school on time. They had no idea it was going to lead me straight down the primrose path.

At this late date it's probably hard to imagine the Rolling Stones having a real presence in someone's life, but there they were: In 1973, "Brown Sugar"—their massive riff on slave girls, cunnilingus, and S&M—was still in heavy rotation. There was a real mystique about the Stones. They were far dirtier, nastier, and just plain more dangerous than *anything*. "Brown Sugar" may seem like some sort of innocuous "classic rock" museum piece now, but it's a real slab of sexual mayhem. It was information from the edge.

Following the Stones across the 1970s, you could pretty much chart my progress from rock 'n' roll curiosity seeker to fully developed delinquent. I remember buying *Sticky Fingers*, the album that "Brown Sugar" came out on, when I was twelve years old. I paid fifty cents for it at a yard sale behind some nice old house on Grandview Avenue (probably the one my mother wanted to move into). Then my friend Eric found a copy of

George Harrison's *All Things Must Pass*, which had three LPs in a box, and I thought he got the better deal. But when we got home, Harrison's boosted Hare Krishna lullabies sounded downright flaccid next to the Stones' twisted-knife love songs "Bitch" and "Sway," not to mention "Sister Morphine" and "Dead Flowers"—all of which sounded like pure freaking *contraband*.

The cover of *Sticky Fingers*, designed by their friend Andy Warhol, is a close-up photo of the crotch of a pair of jeans, with an actual zipper manufactured right into the LP, designed to be pulled down. This was probably my first clue that somewhere, somebody was getting his cock sucked, and it was awesome.

Their double live LP *Love You Live* came out in 1977 when I was fourteen, and I remember seeing the photos from that tour—Mick Jagger was riding something that looked an awful lot like a giant inflatable penis. It was a bit of a mixed signal, but all very nasty in the best possible way. By the time *Some Girls* came out the next year, the Stones were aristocracy, and had been for a while, but the music was sleazier than ever. They gave me the idea that I could become a gentleman outlaw and still harbor perfectly filthy thoughts.

11

BROTHERS AND SISTERS

O ur last great shared moment—my father and I—was July 20, 1969, when he woke me up to watch the first man land on the moon. I remember it clear as a bell, sitting on the edge of my parents' bed, with its soft, blue summer cotton sheets, staring at the black-and-white Philco® television set. The blurry image moved haltingly across the screen, and the crackling audio percolated from the tiny speaker, the first transmission from another world.

I was in love with the space program, agape with the gauzy optimism of exploration, gaga for the gadgetry and gee-whiz of NASA. I still reminisce about the blue NASA jumpsuit I had my picture taken in when I was eight, and about how I wanted to be a space captain and have sex with Barbarella and all of her friends when I was sixteen. After watching the first man land on the moon, my mind was racing with possibilities, because even at the cusp of my fifth birthday, I was a man with a vision. Well, that's my version of it. Others might say I was a hopeless dreamer.

Looking back, I have come to realize the fundamental difference between how I saw the first moon landing and how my father saw it: He saw expensive hardware and American exceptionalism. I saw adventure. I saw rockets and stars. He wanted to meet the astronauts and ask them what it was like to walk on the moon. I wanted to go there and find out for myself.

THE 1970S WERE A GREAT TIME to grow up. It felt wide open, as if anything could happen. I remember catching a Frisbee® at a David Bowie concert in 1978 during his *"Heroes"* (aka "Isolar II") tour, which may or may not sound like a major life event, but it was a *very* big deal. Rock concerts were *happenings*, and tossing disks and beach balls through the giant cumulus clouds of marijuana smoke that filled up the arena while everyone was waiting for the lights to go down was an important part of the trip.

For David Bowie in 1978, everyone had really stepped up their act. Women came *dressed* to this revival meeting, with tons of glitter makeup, hot pants, platform boots, and tight *Diamond Dogs* T-shirts faded from the previous tour. A lot of the guys came out sporting the *Aladdin Sane* lightning-bolt face paint. It was as if Jesus had fallen to Earth.

The girl that asked me to go to the show with her was wearing denim overalls and no shirt. The bib and straps somehow managed to cover her nipples, and her breasts just hung there, flawlessly, like some sort of middle finger in the face of gravity. Even in this crowd, she nearly caused a riot. I have no idea why I was invited. There were four of us, and I was the youngest. She held my hand when we got off the train and made it to our seats on the arena floor.

Anyway, I caught a Frisbee. You always kind of hoped that one would come your way, and that if it did you could be quick enough to catch it. It was a lot more badass than just swatting at a beach ball. But before I could fling it back, the guy next to me said, "Wait a sec," and then took it from me, flipped it over, and poured a big pile of sparkling white powder on it. We all snorted a line, and then I let it sail. And let me tell you: I can throw a Frisbee with the best of them. It is one of the five things I do really well.

I don't know if you've ever had a chance to huck a Frisbee across the arena at Madison Square Garden, but it is truly something else. There is a lot of space, and you can really air it out. With what turned out to be wonderfully pure amphetamine percolating across my brain, and David Bowie about to start the show, it was one of the finest, most crystalline moments of the entire decade. That was me living in the extreme present.

I GOT LUCKY and caught a good wave—the tail end of an era of bewildered enlightenment. Only four years behind me, my brothers got hammered with the dawn of a new dark age.

They graduated high school in 1986. Reagan had been president since they were twelve, and would be until they were twenty. The year they got to college, the so-called Rock and Roll Hall of Fame was just opening its doors, a spectacular cultural landgrab and cynical deification of all that had once been dismissed by the establishment as dirty and unholy. The corporate hippies who ran the joint began, innocently enough, by embracing old-school rockers like Elvis and Fats Domino, and it was all terribly quaint. But before you could say *Yo! Bum Rush the Show*, they were co-opting punk rock and hip-hop, and the message became very clear: As a mode of expression, rebellion was now tragically outdated. Even the new Stones' records were more about attracting corporate sponsors than sexual partners. Their last big hit, "Start Me Up," a perfectly nonthreatening midtempo arena rocker, sounded as if it were recorded in a bank. One thing you could say about Mick Jagger, he was always a man of his times.

My brothers and their pals derisively called me "vintage" because they thought I was hopelessly stuck in the 1960s. They were neither freaks nor geeks, and would have made for good background in any of the John Hughes movies of the day. I actually have no idea what their dreams are, or were. As far as I know, when they were in high school they didn't hang out and play "lawyer" or "investment banker" with their friends. Certainly they weren't snorting mystery dust off Frisbees at David Bowie concerts.

I was definitely the outlier in this group, but we grew up in the same house. We had the same parents and listened to the same fights. We ate the same shitty frozen kosher turkey breast. So, why are we so different? Because they were too young to remember seeing a grown man do his best impersonation of a nuclear meltdown just because someone ordered a meatball pizza?

My brothers are twins—they spent nine months in the womb with their asses in each other's faces. One of them is clearly more like my parents—reserved and conservative in his taste—whereas the other was always just a bit more gung ho for thrills (for a while he dated a girl in high school who smoked cigarettes *and* drove a white Camaro®). But they both became family guys with all the fixin's. Given our family dysfunction, one has to wonder where they found anything attractive in that lifestyle, but they love their children relentlessly. They might be a little confused about who I am, but there is no meanness about them. And mostly they got along well with my folks, especially my dad. It probably didn't hurt that, like my parents, they grew up at a time when rebellion had little value as any sort of viable currency.

My mom is also a twin, and she could not be more different from her twin brother, who is pretty much her opposite number: wildly confident and successful, seemingly impervious to any sort of setback. My dad's sister, ditto, is nothing at all like him. Seven years younger than him, she is the only other person in the family who could be considered a rebel, and she is one of the most admirable people I have the privilege to know. She is the only person I know personally of whom it can be said, "She saved a lot of lives."

Like my father, she attended an expensive Boston prep school that funneled into an elite university, although when I was a kid I heard rumors that she had been thrown out of college for having a motorcycle, which naturally sent her stock through the roof. I remember seeing a black-and-white photograph of her from those days, maybe 1963. She was wearing a black sweater and posing with a black cat. She had long black hair and looked like Joan and Mimi Baez's younger, prettier sister—the perfect beatnik chick.

"That story is overblown," she always told me. "It was my boyfriend's bike, and it wasn't supposed to be on campus. That's it. Not a big deal. I was only a rebel because I wore weird clothes. But I was successful, so no one bothered me. I got A's in school. I got a good job. I accomplished what *they* wanted."

After a very successful career in advertising, she dropped out of the corporate world to run her own adventure travel company, working closely with the indigenous tribal people and nomads of western Africa. Eventually she gave that up to work exclusively on outreach and charity, building schools and water purification facilities, bringing medicine and cattle to Mali, Niger, and Ethiopia, for example.

One afternoon a few years ago she called me on the phone to ask me if I had ever heard of the band Led Zeppelin.

"I think they were popular when I was in high school," I deadpanned. "Why would you like to know?"

"Oh, I met this man, Robert Plant, in Mali when I was there working. Apparently he is their singer. He was there doing some music, and he wrote me a very generous check for my charity."

"That was very nice of him," I said.

About a week later she called me again.

"Have you ever heard of a song called 'Stairway to Heaven'?"

"I think it was popular when I was in high school," I deadpanned.

"Oh," she said, "I thought since he was so nice to give me money for my charity that I should buy one of his records . . . and it is just lovely!" At which point I dropped the charade and told her the gospel of Led Zeppelin, a band so epic in sound, scope, and popularity that I did not know a single person whose lives they did not touch. I tried to explain the myth and mystique of "Stairway to Heaven," but she had no idea what I was talking about. She was just thrilled that the guy who sang it was supportive of her relief efforts in Mali. I could not possibly have been more proud of her—that sound you hear is me *kvelling*, with "Kashmir" playing in the background.

But my father was embarrassed by her. She still wears "weird clothes," favoring African fabrics and jewelry from her many trips there, and she is still and always stunningly beautiful. She is one of those rare people who enter a room and everyone's game gets better. But Dad never boasted of her, and on at least one occasion, at a fund-raiser for her charity that he sheepishly attended, he actually pretended not to know her.

"It was our mother who made your father what he was. When we were kids, she wanted everyone to judge her by how perfect her children were. She made us put on little outfits and bring everyone drinks. That's where your father got it. You were an embarrassment to him. When he told you off at the end, he knew exactly what he was doing. He was determined to destroy you."

I had to say, even for my father, that seemed a bit harsh.

"Your success was not the kind that he admired. The magazines you worked on were an embarrassment to him. He hated your freedom," she told me, echoing a common sentiment among people who knew both my father and me. "When you took off with your band, going someplace *just because you wanted to*? He despised you for that.

"I was rigid, just like him," she confessed. "It took me forever to learn that *everyone* is perfect.

"He yelled at me for not coming to see him when he was sick. But he never told me he *was* sick. He *never* told me he had *cancer*, and he lived with it for *years*. I never knew. But then he told me *not* to come see him, because he didn't want anyone to ever see him not wearing a blue blazer and gray pants. It was nonsense, but wearing that outfit was his source of authority."

It was a costume, of course: his blazer, slacks, and bow tie, the logical prêt-à-porter for a kayfabe superhero whose power emanated from a canny ability to prove superiority through studied but clearly affluent understatement. Sartorially, at least, he was topping from the bottom.

Proof of his dominion came when he showed up to Brother No. 2's wedding in his "perfect preppy" outfit. My mother was nearly apoplectic, spitting that "a man should wear a suit at a wedding."

12

MOM

A few years after my father died, a funny thing happened: My mother died.

Okay, that's not funny, but as any writer will tell you, genuine irony is a rare bird indeed, and that's what we're talking about here. This story has a happy ending.

Mom was a lot more like my father than she would ever have admitted: He wanted everything to be perfect and turned his back on everything that wasn't, which was most of the world. Children meant scrapes and bruises and fights and dirt and messes and broken hearts, and he didn't want to deal with any of it. Neither did Mom. I don't know where she got the idea that it was all going to be easy, but once she got it in her head that she was a victim of my father's bullying, she began to take everything personally.

But my mother was never mean to me, and in her own way, as she got farther and farther away from my father emotionally, she was actually supportive. She had no real understanding of what I did ("Can people really buy your books?"), but she just wanted the best for her kids. "If you ever need anything you can call me," she would always say, and I think she genuinely thought that I was going to make that call.

For years she saw my life—no matter what job I had, no matter whom I was dating, no matter where I lived, no matter how happy I was—as a continuous downward slide. Unlike my old man, if I were in jail, she would have bailed me out first and asked questions later. Of course, then I'd have to listen to her click her tongue at me, which is how Jewish mothers signal displeasure to their children. It's a tribal thing. And then there's the Sigh of the Martyr ("Why are you doing this to *me*?"), and thinking about it now, jail would probably be the preferable option. Anyway, I have my lawyer on speed dial in the eventuality that I do get arrested, for whatever (hopefully a good First Amendment case). But anyway, what's important is that, even with all of the frustration and disappointment, she never once rooted *against* me.

She had been coughing a bit, and when she went in to get an X-ray. They found a spot on her lung, so she got on the phone and told her kids, and then everyone she knew.

A week later, after a biopsy revealed everyone's worst fear—Stage IV lung cancer—she was back on the phone, tearfully telling everyone that she was going to beat it.

In stark contrast with my dad, she started writing mass, open emails to everyone with whom she had ever played tennis or golf, everyone at her country club, detailing her chemotherapy and every detail of her battle. She wanted to make her cancer a group experience.

At first she fought like a Viking, a real country-club warrior, playing nine holes of golf in the morning and swimming in the afternoon on Monday, eighteen holes on Tuesday, followed by a dinner party, and on and on. It all left her exhausted, but clearly she had something to prove. "I'm so tired," she would tell me when she called me at night to check in, "but *we're* gonna beat this thing."

I told her that even for someone in tip-top shape, it would be pretty normal to be exhausted after days like that, especially in the wilting Florida heat. It was an odd strain of martyrdom—not the "being sick" part, but the part where you push yourself to limits any healthy person would find draining and then complain at the end of the day, "I'm so tired." She had a long history of not being her own best friend.

It didn't take terribly long for the eighteen-hole days to stop and the swimming to drop off, with a few long walks being the last refuge for a woman who was once a terrific athlete. She had been a vicious tennis player, often winning club and town championships, and she was a natural, gifted golfer. That was her entire life, aside from her grandchildren, whom she doted on as much as they would tolerate. She didn't celebrate Elton John or meatball pizza or anything like that. She never, as far as I know, thought about art or God. There was not a lot of caprice or laughter in her life.

Down in Florida, where as a suburban Jewish-mom-turned-golf-course-grandma it was her genetic imperative to die, she lived in a gated community with a warren of like-minded northern refugees, surrounding a clubhouse that provided a small retreat from the pawnshops, bail bondsmen, closed abortion clinics, and blacked-out windows of what I presumed to be meth labs that dotted the Florida landscape ad infinitum. It was like *The Flintstones*, where the background kept repeating itself—rock, bigger rock, cactus, rock, bigger rock, cactus, rock, etc.—except in Florida the background was Denny's®, pawnshop, meth lab . . . . And once you got inside the gates of "The Oasis West," or whatever precious name they gave her prefab community, the monotony continued. Everything—the houses, the cars, the people—looked *exactly* the same. It felt like the set of a movie about a suburb about to be attacked by space aliens. Oddly, it wasn't all that different from where my father lived in Arizona. His was just the pricier terra-cotta version, carved out of the desert rather than a swamp, and it was called some sort of "Ranch," which was as perfectly preposterous as my mother's place being called an "Oasis," because calling something "something" certainly didn't make it that thing.

It's probably no wonder that for years I visited her only sporadically, even though for most of the year, when she wasn't wintering in Florida, we lived just a short train ride away from each other—me in Manhattan, she in New Jersey.

It's terrible, I know. Taking a thirty-five-minute ride to see my mom seemed like a major *schlep*, but when I was in high school I never thought twice about getting on that same train in the other direction to go to the city to score a Muddy Waters record. Then again, Muddy Waters never yelled at me. Muddy Waters never called me fat. Muddy Waters never clicked his tongue and talked to me through his teeth.

When I got older and got over myself, I would visit her as often as she liked, because if there were a chance it would make her happy, who was I to deny her that joy? And it wasn't really *that* hard to make the trip, as long as I didn't have to go to her house, which was basically one giant white sofa that no one could sit on for fear that they might get it dirty and then get yelled at.

So I'd take the train down to see her, and she'd pick me up at the station and drive us over to the nearest shopping mall and make a grand production of buying me a new shirt, the one activity that we had ever successfully shared that lasted more than a few minutes before one or both of us lost our patience. I mean, you couldn't eat lunch with her—she was weight-obsessed and always dieting. If you went to the food court in the mall with her, there was one allowable choice: *salad*. I once made an error on the play by ordering a turkey sandwich, and she made me get rid of the bread. I remember the time I made the mistake of going to her house for Thanksgiving—my brothers were going, and she insisted on seeing us all together. She leaned over my plate and, scolding me like a toddler, put back some of the turkey I had just served myself, pushed the gravy away from me, and with a dirty look told me, "*You* don't need any potatoes." And then she shut down dinner before dessert, because "You certainly don't need any pie, either."

I tried to escape, going out to the backyard with my brothers to drink more and *kvetch*, but she followed, and after a short round of tongue clicking she started in with, "When are you going to settle down, Michael?" She took it very personally that I wasn't married and hadn't spawned any grandchildren for her.

But you don't get to be that much of a harpy without some blowback, and so I ribbed her a little bit. "C'mon, Mom, tell me the truth—which would you rather: if I came home with a nice Jewish *boy*, or a nice black *girl*?"

"Don't start with me, Michael," she growled, incisors clenched.

Going shirt shopping with her was a lot more pleasant, a sort of micro-economic jihad. You would have marveled at the way she worked a scattergun's worth of coupons secreted in her Prada bag to create new discounts for items already on sale, with mathematical combinations and permutations that no one in the history of department stores had ever imagined. Hers was a gorgeous, Jewy, calculus kung fu that conjured images of an ancient Chinese man whipping beads across an abacus with a long, jeweled fingernail. Watching her work, you knew you were in the presence of a master—someone who was clearly the best at what they did, like Michael Jordan or Jimi Hendrix. She was the Garry Kasparov of coupons. Her technique astonished even the wizened old ladies at the cash register who thought they had seen it all, but who were so dazzled by this blizzard of next-level mall-math that they were practically giving *her* money for a shirt originally marked sixty-five dollars. Come to think of it, she was probably the one who put Gimbels out of business.

But without any sort of retail magic to keep us on the straight and narrow, visiting her in Florida became an echo chamber for everything that was wrong about me for the last forty-plus years. Brother No. 1 had the same experience when he went to visit her by himself. Mostly he had to listen to her moan for twenty-four hours as she guilted him for not visiting more with his kids, and when you are in a small house with a cancer patient, and outside it is 110 degrees and 90 percent humidity, you really don't have much of a choice but to suck it up. Which is okay, because we weren't there on vacation, we were there to try and cheer up our mom. And we were on our best behavior. But that didn't mean we *had* to be miserable, too, did it?

When he got back home, he called me and we compared notes and decided to do the next visit together, since then at least we'd have each other to talk to. And anyway, my mother always said that she loved it when her children spent time together—it made her feel like we were "more of a family." And so we coordinated planes from different cities to meet in the West Palm Beach airport and show up bright and shiny and happy, together.

The night we arrived, my brother and I, as instructed, went to get take-out food for dinner. We took her car and on the way stopped at a liquor store to get some wine that we thought might pair well with the bucket of veal parmigiana and spaghetti that her husband insisted we get at "New York Style Italian Restaurant."

No kidding, that was the actual name of the place, "New York Style Italian Restaurant"—and you can be quite sure, anywhere in the world, that the more a restaurant claims to be "New York style," the less it will be. Some people will never figure out the difference between spaghetti with marinara sauce and egg noodles with ketchup. Just ask Henry Hill.

On the way back, we realized that if we tried to bring *two* bottles of wine into the house, we were going to get yelled at. As it was, we got yelled at for the first bottle:

> **MOM**: How much did you spend on that?
>
> **BROTHER (KAYFABE)**: Twelve dollars.
>
> **MOM (ANGRY, CLICKING TONGUE)**: If that's the way you want to waste your money, go ahead . . .

At first we were going to leave the second bottle in the car and retrieve it later, but I saw that quickly backfiring, like some harebrained scheme on *The Brady Bunch* or *I Love Lucy*. Either she was going to tell her husband to move the car and he'd find it, or we'd get locked out somehow and have to break in, so we decided to hide the wine in the bushes, which was perfectly ridiculous because never mind my own peregrinations, my brother is the managing director of a large financial institution and not only should he *not* be getting the stink-eye for buying a bottle of (kayfabe) twelve-dollar wine, neither should he have any business hiding a bottle of Italian red behind the azaleas—especially on a hundred-degree day. But such was the power of my mother's mojo. Later that night, we sneaked out and drank it on the golf course behind her house, proving once and for all that you can take the boys out of New Jersey, but you can't take the New Jersey out of the boys.

The next day we got yelled at for what I'm not sure, but the new mandate was that she would only permit her children to visit her one at a time. "I can't handle you boys together," she declared, and we both left feeling like our visit had made everyone involved miserable.

The next time out, I got smart and took my new girlfriend—and lo and behold, a *mitzvah* happened.

The first thing the new girlfriend (also a bombshell of a lawyer with artistic inclinations, you'd think I would have learned my lesson) did was turn off the television in my mom's room that had been bleating with the acid tumult of Fox News, a cable television station dedicated to fear (Immigrants! Disease! Terrorism!) and the right-wing fetish for people yelling at one another. "You can't heal with all of this anger in the room," the new girl-friend told her, and she made the screaming heads on the television disappear with a click of the remote.

And then she did *real* magic.

"I love Michael, and I came here to get your blessing," she told my mom. "I am going to love him and make him happy." And then she gave Mom a big squishy hug, and I swear they *glowed*—I took a picture of them with my phone and you could actually see the halo-like aura. It was a real moment. *Beatific*, I believe, is the word. And then I gave Mom a hug, and it was quite mushy all around. Everyone was crying by now: me, the new girl-friend, and Mom, who was melting like a Popsicle® right before our eyes.

IS THERE ANY GREATER BLESSING than to bring another person joy? Especially someone who is dying. This was the greatest gift of all.

My mother had finally let *me* make *her* happy. Never before had I seen her so accepting of love without judg-ment. I know it was the cancer, and the creeping finality of her situation, but the new girlfriend melted her way through all of that noise with real love and sunshine, and all of a sudden Mom was looking at me a lot differently.

And beyond finding this new acceptance, she took a radical turn. For a moment, at least, she became both softer and more self-aware than I had ever seen her. It said a boatload when she told the new girlfriend that I got a raw deal growing up, that I was treated much differently than my brothers were, and that she felt bad about it all. "It shouldn't have been like that," she said, and she was sorry. Sorry! She didn't miss the opportunity to ring up the old man for any number of high crimes and misdemeanors ("his father was a cheap asshole"), but to completely let go of her anger would have been a few standard deviations, at least, away from her conditioned behavior of the last thirty-plus years. No one held on to anger like my mom did.

But this was good. She didn't say any of it to me—not *exactly*. She had to work through a third-party broker, namely the new girlfriend, but it cleared the path for us. From there straight through to the end of our earthly relationship, we had love—love without *shpilkes*! I think she figured I needed someone to take care of me, because *obviously* I wasn't capable of it myself, and finally, she didn't have to worry. The new girlfriend seemed sane. Maybe this was the end of all that playing in bands and writing of books.

"I'm so glad you are finally settling down," she wept, holding the new girlfriend's hand. But what she never got was that there was never going to be any *settling*, and there was definitely no *down*.

ABOUT THAT IRONY, I haven't forgotten.

While I was at Mom's house with the new girlfriend, I called my brothers and left messages saying that against all odds we were having a great visit. A little later Brother No. 2 called Mom and said, "Hey, I heard Michael made your day!" And Mom came back at him with, "MY DAY??? HE MADE MY LIFE!!! I AM SOOOOOOO HAPPY!!!!" I think they heard her in Havana.

Ten minutes later, Brother No. 1 calls *me* and says, "What the fuck? Your brother and I finished college, got good jobs, and married Jewish girls . . . and you show up in the bottom of the ninth, unemployed, with a *shiksa* girlfriend, and *you're* the one she's happy with?"

It's true: No one saw that coming. Sometimes the long shot comes in.

AFTER THAT VISIT, the new girlfriend and I went on a beach vacation together, and I emailed Mom photos every day. We had fun, glamming up our selfies to look like movie stars, with our sunglasses and Panama hats—but no cocktails, because I knew she wouldn't approve of that. Mom couldn't get enough. She responded to every ridiculous photo and my stupid captions with great enthusiasm—"She's so beautiful, I am so happy for you!"—until she could no longer sit up to type, and the messages stopped.

Her home health-care aide told us she wasn't going to open her eyes again. The morphine drip had taken her into a quiet, faraway place. But she was able to listen, so we called her every morning and afternoon to tell her that we loved her, all the while trying to mute our crying, because let me tell you, that is one tough fucking call to make, telling your unconscious mother that you love her through a speakerphone.

The nurse usually told us, "She heard you, she squeezed my hand."

And then that, too, stopped, and she was gone.

She was so small and frail when she died. The cancer just ate at her. It probably wouldn't have hurt her to have eaten some of that veal parmigiana, but by then it was too late.

For a while she had been going to her club to play cards with the ladies wearing a wig, after the chemo knocked the hair off her head, but at some point she just started going out without it. Finally she had found enough brass to say, "Look, this is who I am, and I know it's not perfect, but if I can deal with it, then so can you." I told her, "Hey, I lost my hair a long time before you did, and I'm still rocking." That may have been the first joke of mine she ever laughed at.

I WROTE MOM'S OBITUARY for her local newspaper and eulogized her with all the might I could muster, in front of what had to be considered a pretty good crowd. I think about two hundred people came to her funeral—more than have come to any of my gigs in a while.

As I've said, I always strive to be a *mensch*, but I also strive to be honest. And I promise you that giving a speech leaning over the box your dead mother is in is no picnic. Fortunately, somehow, I was reminded of the cocaine penis. I always felt like that was our dirty little secret, unspoken, but something we had shared on another plane of consciousness, and it forced me to remember that no matter her shortcomings, my mom was human, and an adult, and she dealt with all sorts of weird shit, the same as we all do. I know, it's just awful— my poor mother just died of cancer, and I've got this scene of erections and disco dust dancing through my head—but privately it made me laugh and kept me from blubbering through the eulogy. The cocaine penis kept me *strong*.

This is what I said:

"For the first three years of my life, me and my mom got along great."

That got a few nervous laughs, mostly from my brothers, who had the same look that comes when the plane you are on hits a scary patch of turbulence. The only thing you can do is look around and see if the flight attendants are scared. I shot a glance at the rent-a-rabbi, and she was cool, so I moved on. "After that . . ." I trailed off and shrugged, guiltily. It is a good skill to have, shrugging guiltily. The whys and wherefores are often better left unsaid.

"But in the end, despite it all, we shared the greatest blessing imaginable—*shpilke*s were out, *kvelling* was in!"

BIG points for throwing down the Yiddish. I was, as we say in the wrestling biz, *over*. The old Jews were eating it up. For a change, I was working *babyface*.

"My mom and I were finally able to find joy in each other's lives and share a great happiness. What she wanted, simply, was the best for me, as she did for my brothers—who by the way, were the direct beneficiaries of my teenage prevarications. What was bad for the goose turned out to be pretty good for the gander. After my shenanigans, they could have robbed a bank and still come out looking like cupcakes."

Thumbs up and tears from siblings. Laughter from her country-club pals.

"My mom was very good at what she did. She was a fantastic elementary school teacher," I beamed, "and her kids loved her as she loved them. She won awards. Once she dressed up as the letter *A* on Halloween, which was the silliest thing I have ever seen her do, but she did it because it was her job to teach kids how to read—the single most important job in the world.

"And, as everyone who knew her knew well, she was a ferocious tennis player, a true champion, and a fantastic and dedicated golfer. She hit an astonishing seven holes in one. But she took it in stride, because the most important thing in her life was never personal achievement or awards; it was just the joy she took in her kids and her grandkids.

"Of course, like any good Jewish mom, it often came out as worrying. But this was the way she expressed her love, and in the end all we had was love, because truly, love is who we are. And that's who my mom was."

After that speech about a hundred old ladies, my mom's mah-jongg partners and golf pals and extended circle of *yentas*, all made it a point to tell me how happy I had made her. And then a few days *after* the funeral, I got a letter from her. She had written one for each of her children, to be mailed upon her death.

It was cast on an old page of three-ringed notebook paper that she must have been saving for fifteen years, since she last worked as a schoolteacher. Niceties like fancy stationery were a waste of money to her. I can't remember how many times I got yelled at for buying cards for her (another thing she had in common with the old man), never mind presents, because she didn't want me spending my money. Flowers were a big no-no. "It's a waste," she always said, "because they die." She was always a bit of a scold, but I found her unwillingness to accept gifts from her children as particularly selfish. I think in her mind it somehow weakened the position she had staked out as a victim in life, but it also took joy away from those who wanted to do something nice for her.

The letter arrived while I was packing up my apartment, getting ready to move—the new girlfriend and I were going to play house, and I was keeping with the program and meditating on how happy it would have made my mom to see us in our new place together. Of course I had never purposely tried to make either of my parents *unhappy*, but given their rigid expectations, it was a pretty safe bet that's exactly what was going to happen, just like when a monkey goes into a bakery, you can be pretty sure it is not going to end well. This was definitely better. Premeditated disappointment had served no one.

I was just about to take a walk to the local pub to get a cold beer—I had been choking on fifteen years of dust and cat dander and needed a break—and I took her missive with me. Ever the romantic, I thought that sitting alone over a glass of something strong (the moment the envelope arrived, I upgraded from beer to whiskey) while reading an honest-to-goodness letter was the way to go. When's the last time anyone sent you a *letter*, never mind one from *beyond the grave*? It was downright *gothic*. What pearls of wisdom would she impart? This was her legacy on blue-lined paper!

Well, it wasn't quite like that.

"You were my first born, and I loved you with all my heart," it began. "But somehow you got off the beaten path. You really strayed. The hardest day of my life was when you dropped out of school."

Really, Mom? Worse than getting divorced? Worse than watching your parents die? Worse than the day they told you that you had lung cancer?? Good Lord, if I had known my folks were going to take that to the grave with them as my single most noteworthy accomplishment, I might have re-enrolled and dropped out a few more times.

The letter concluded, "I think you are finally on the right course." But of course she couldn't leave it there, adding, "It took you fifty years, but it was worth it." You have to hand it to her for setting the bar pretty freaking high in the Jewish guilt department—whipping that out after you're already dead is some real heavyweight shit.

"Both of your parents," Dr. Headshrinker told me, "were looking for *you* to fulfill *their* needs, not the other way around, which is what should happen in a healthy parent-child relationship—certainly at least until you are an adult. They were both selfish like that . . . They had a very specific narrative that they expected you to fill, and when you didn't, they blamed you for the deficits in their own lives. Your father wanted you to be just like him, but probably not quite as successful, so he could still feel superior. Your mother wasn't so insidious—she just wanted a storybook. Either way, you, being who you are, were destined to fail in their eyes, no matter how successful at life you actually were."

I looked at the date on the letter and it was written a few weeks before Mom met the new girlfriend and we had our shared epiphany, so I gave her a pass and clung to our newfound mother-son bliss and her love for me, which had always been there but had been twisted completely out of shape, what with the travails of a strain of suburban strife for which she was in no way prepared.

Anyway, how can you fault someone who is dying? I mean if they don't use their last breath to bury you? I felt like crying, but I kept a lid on it because I was in a bar after all, and didn't want to be that weird Jewish guy weeping in the corner.

The truly strange thing is that I miss her all the time now. I never thought I would, but now every time I am overeating, or spend too much money on a shirt, I think about how she would be clicking her tongue in disapproval, like an African tribesman, if only she could see me.

FROM MAULER TO MAHLER

One of my aging relatives told me that if there were one person I absolutely needed to talk to while writing about my father, it was, in fact, my father, and she knew someone who could put me in touch with him, no problem. I politely told her, "No thank you." For the time being, at least, I was going to stick to traditional reporting methods.

But she pressed ahead, and left me numerous messages—she had been in touch with him via a psychic, and he had a message for me.

The idea of using a medium to get in touch with dead people seems, to use my favorite word, *icky*. Who's to say if they have a DO NOT DISTURB sign up on their doors? Do they have voice mail in the afterlife?

It was particularly upsetting when it came to my father. On Earth he was a closeted unhappy person.

Maybe now he was free to be unhappy all the time, which would make me terribly sad, because I truly hope that he is in a better place. But either way, why should I go chasing his ghost? I saw nothing good coming from reaching across the vale of tears, such as it was, to talk to my father. There was a good chance he wasn't done yelling at me.

I made a thousand excuses not to return the calls, but at some point I had to call her back, because not to would have been rude. And, apparently, he had a message for me. "He can see more clearly now what you are trying to do," she told me.

That was it? No apology? He didn't want to finally say, *Gee, son, I'm proud of you*?

And now, goddammit, look at me, all in a twist *because a psychic whom I do not believe in, and did not want to hear from in the first place, delivers me a message from my dead father*—and I am disappointed in the content?

Good grief.

She added that she was frequently in touch with her mother—they spoke all the time—and that this new cross-dimensional relationship had really been helpful to both of them, and that I should really make an effort to talk to my father across the abyss. I thanked her again but declined to take the number of her psychic.

I suppose if there really were spirits who felt like visiting, the sleeping brain would be a fertile field for them to make landfall, kind of like a bar where everyone knows your name. Maybe the dream state is like the Internet for dead people—a good place to cruise for family and friends. It's probably much easier to drift into a dream than to start rattling chains or writing messages on foggy mirrors or dusty walls. For a dead person, that is probably a giant pain in the ass.

One dead friend of mine showed up in a dream recently. He was one of my best friends and died when I was about thirty. I knew him since we were eighteen. It was a suicide. His death broke my heart, and I dedicated my first book to him. I still keep a picture of him hanging in my living room: a black-and-white photograph I took of him playing in his punk rock band in a Bedford-Stuyvesant loft in about 1983. I printed it myself in the NYU dark room.

He looked pretty good in the dream—more or less the same as I remembered him—and he thanked me for thinking about him. I asked him what it's like where he was. "It's okay," he said. "The people here are nice." It was comforting to hear, and the whole dream was so entirely *not* weird, and pleasant, that it would be easy enough to believe.

When I dream about my father, he's also just as I remember him in better days. He criticizes me, and we get into petty fights right away. I search for approval, and then I feel crappy when I don't get it. Not much has changed. In the most recent dream I asked him to read something, and he said, "No, I'm not interested." And then I told him don't worry, it's not something I wrote, I'm just trying to share something nice I saw in the paper. And then he showed slightly more interest.

It was an obituary of a friend of mine who had recently died, a really lovely write-up of a woman I knew—a journalist who had broken through the old-school boys club of the newspaper racket and was something of a local legend—and he said, "Why would I believe a word of it? I am sure it is all about the writer. These things always are." I woke up thinking that wherever he is, he is not going to be very happy about this book of mine.

In another dream, he told me that *he* was going to write a book. I told him jokingly (the same way I rib a lot of people who get the idea that they want to write a book), "Don't do it! It always seems like a good idea, but it's such a *schlep*. It's like having homework every day for a year." (After half a dozen books, I can testify this is true enough.) He told me, "You never were any good at doing your homework. That's probably why your books aren't very good."

* * *

WHEN I WAS TWENTY-FIVE YEARS OLD, I owned exactly one "classical" music record, Glenn Gould's 1955 version of Bach's *The Goldberg Variations*, which I bought because a Canadian girl I was keen on told me I needed to listen to it. When it came to the classical music thing, I was right off the turnip truck. Glenn Gould, apparently, was like the Wayne Gretzky of the piano.

I played the Gould occasionally and enjoyed it, but I never got any action from the girl, and the record faded into the rest of my collection. Who knows: If she had slept with me, I'd probably be playing the *Brandenburg Concertos* on a harpsichord by now instead of continuing to hammer away at Bo Diddley on an electric guitar.

About fifteen years after that, I went to see the first *Jackass* movie, which, if you recall, was hardly a movie at all, but more like a series of slapstick vignettes, each more perverse and violent than what came before it, and generally loathed by what one would call "people of taste." The *Jackass* guys loved to fire bottle rockets out of their butts, zap one another with stun guns, ride their skateboards at high speeds into brick walls (because somehow that is hilarious), cover themselves in steaks and fight off hungry Dobermans, play demolition derby in golf carts, etc. It was impressive how much pain these guys were willing to withstand for a cheap laugh.

The first scene of the first *Jackass* movie (such was the popularity of stoners electrocuting one another for a few yuks that these movies actually became a successful franchise) featured the entire cast of wounded misfits hurtling down the side of a mountain in a giant shopping cart while bombs exploded around them. Eventually they went sailing off a cliff, Wile E. Coyote–style.

Adding to the laughs was the soundtrack: a bombastic choral symphony blasted at rock-concert volume. Clearly someone's idea of irony, it helped transform the willful idiocy of these morons into a demented ballet of sorts—and right then I decided that I should spend more time listening to bombastic symphonies, putting Beethoven at the top of my "To Do" list.

As I like to say, sometimes you just have to take it where you find it—and if the most reviled comic troupe of no-brain masochists in the world was going to be my entry point into classical music, so be it. I hear it, I like it, I look for more. Like I've said before: Curiosity killed the cat, but satisfaction brought him back. Now tell me, how many more lives do I have left?

It was just like being a teenager all over again, getting up and out to discover all of this wonder for myself. I really had no idea what I was doing—that Beethoven cat made a lot of records! So I started out with what I thought, based on reputation, were going to be the biggest and baddest: Beethoven's Fifth and Ninth Symphonies; Brahms's Symphony No. 4; and Mozart's Symphonies Nos. 40 and 41, and of course there were like fifty versions of each one, by various orchestras and conductors, and who the hell knew what the difference was; and also Carl Orff's opus, *Carmina Burana*, which is what I had unearthed as the choral swarm wailing on the *Jackass* soundtrack. You would recognize it from luxury car commercials, or possibly a satanic possession film, if you went in for that sort of thing.

I also picked up a disk of Beethoven's piano sonatas, because I figured they would have a lot of what I came to call "the Bugs Bunny Quotient," defined casually as the kind of thing that would cause wild gesticulating if played or conducted by a cartoon rabbit wearing a top hat and tails. Never mind the BBQ—which it delivered in spades, the "Moonlight" and the "Waldstein" especially—what I didn't expect was to be frozen by the abject beauty of Beethoven's solo piano work. Each composition seemed to tell an epic story. About what? I have no fucking idea. There was no *real* narrative here, not in the "poor boy from Illinois grows up to be president and frees the slaves" kind of way, but those sonatas sure took you for a ride. As you might stick your nose in a glass of wine and get notes of plums or a bit of leather, I listened to these and got stormy seas and rough sex. There was nearly unbearable tension and release, preternatural calm, divine mystery, and explosive joy, all expressed in music so expansive that mere words wilt in its presence. Is that too earnest? Fuck it: I was floored.

The recording of piano sonatas I picked up was by Maurizio Pollini on the Deutsche Grammophon® label, for no other reason than it was the first one in the bin, and I understood that DG was something like the Stiff Records of the classical world, a name you could trust. I played it over and over and over again. Nothing had really captivated me like this since the first time I heard Chuck Berry play "Johnny B. Goode" on the *American Graffiti* soundtrack (which also came out during the annus mirabilis of '73). Pretty soon I was sitting on a pretty big pile of classical records, which you could still buy stacks of at the Salvation Army® for a quarter a pop. And when Pollini came to town, I was lucky to get quite literally the very last ticket available in Carnegie Hall—in the very top row in the balcony, in the most remote corner of the entire venue—to see him.

It was a beautiful spring Sunday afternoon, and I gaily ran uptown to get there early enough to smoke half a joint in Central Park on top of my favorite rock. After getting a drink in the lounge just off the lobby, I found my seat at precisely two p.m., since unlike impudent jazzers and rockers, I had a feeling these classical cats liked to start right on time.

Two o'clock came and went. Two twenty, two twenty-five . . .

"He must be getting a cut of the bar," I said to the fellow sitting next to me, who was tapping his watch impatiently. But he didn't laugh. And this is where I learned that you are not supposed to make jokes at these things—which is kind of a drag. Why do classical music fans have to be so goddam serious? No wonder the median age at Carnegie Hall was about a thousand.

It was a few weeks after having my brain zorched by Pollini's turn at the *Appassionata* that the editors of one of the local arts weeklies approached me. They had really liked my first book, which had recently come out, and wanted to know if I would consider writing for them. I agreed, on one condition: I was only willing to write about professional wrestling and classical music. Okay, so two conditions. But for some reason, they agreed.

I had an idea to work an angle with the classical music. I could never approach the subject with the authority of say, the *New York Times* classical music guys, and would only make an ass of myself if I tried. So I came at it with an unhinged sort of enthusiasm, with the idea to write about classical music in rock 'n' roll terms, for the folks who didn't go out to classical concerts because they

figured it was going to be performed by codgers in pow-
dered wigs.

I advocated that the hipster nation get good and
stoned and sit front and center for Mozart's Symphony
No. 25 in G minor—what I like to call "the Sonic Reducer
Symphony," because the opening riff of the symphony
(the first music heard in the movie *Amadeus*) sounds a
hell of a lot like the Dead Boys' minor punk rock masterpiece. Have a go at them both, and tell me I am wrong.

My preview of a Mahler cycle was a thinly disguised
run at Pink Floyd:

> "A symphony must be like the world. It must
> contain everything," Mahler famously said, but
> by no means did he embrace the kitchen-sink
> worldview later perpetrated by over-reaching
> art rock bands, throwing in every gloop and gleep
> one can possibly make by twisting the knobs on a
> Mini Moog, confusing syrup with sentiment and
> bombast with importance. Mahler's work puts
> into sharp contrast the kind of contrived angst
> that sourpusses like Pink Floyd have made a
> career of by capturing and expanding on *genuine*
> feelings of dread, sadness, joy, and redemption—
> to name but four—and without the aid of
> inflatable pigs, laser light shows, and idiotic,

ham-fisted "wall" metaphors that were tired long before Thomas Jefferson wrote to the Danbury Baptists.

I guess ripping Pink Floyd meant I was working as a heel—at least in some circles—but as "Rowdy" Roddy Piper once told me, it is always the heels who sell tickets. Anyway, I was totally "over" with the publicists and press agents who handled classical music concerts in New York. They were ga-ga for my gimmick, which meant plenty of comped tickets.

But, to the point: Later in his life, my father also became enthusiastic about classical music, although you can be sure his path had been quite different from mine (no stoners stun-gunning one another for laughs), and I tried very hard to engage him on the topic. I thought maybe—finally—we had reached some common ground, and that hopefully our relationship could take a right turn onto some friendly turf. Surely he would approve of my own good taste!

I was practically groveling for some respect. A nod, a wink, some father-son bonhomie—anything. *Look! I have culture, too! Now maybe it will be okay to like me!* Maybe a bit of Brahms or Borodin was just the salve we were missing? I have to imagine that he felt it, too. Haven't we grown up, at all?

As usual, I blew it. I mentioned that I had begun writing about classical music for the local paper, which, in New York City, was a pretty big coup. I thought parents were supposed to be proud of stuff like that.

"You know, I've been going to the symphony a lot lately," I told him, after listening to him boast how great the weather was in Arizona, and with such fierce pride that you'd think he was somehow responsible for it himself. Places that still had winter were below his station.

"Oh really," he wagered. "I thought you were into punk rock."

"I'm into all sorts of things, you know. But I've really been loving going to see the symphony, and writing about it. It's a great gig."

"Classical music is an expensive hobby," he sniffed, the same way he had so generously helped me with my photography, the message being: *You should quit now.*

What I should have quit doing was trying to find something we could talk about. That was a brushback pitch, and if I didn't stop crowding the plate, the next one was coming at my head. But you know me: I can hardly stop myself.

"Well," I said, "The *radio* is still free. But since I've been working for the newspaper, the publicists and press agents have been super nice to me. Anyway, even when I don't get comped, the cheap seats at Carnegie are great.

Even upstairs in the balcony it sounds fantastic. It's not like Avery Fisher Hall . . ."

And right there, I stepped in it by having the temerity to criticize that great playground of the aristocracy, the former Avery Fisher Hall (now known as David Geffen Hall), the airport-like cavern in Lincoln Center where the New York Philharmonic saws at their fiddles.

I am not the first person, not by a long shot, to question the acoustics at Avery Fisher. They were notoriously bad—the topic of much discussion and expensive attempts at course correction. Basically, the room is just too big. There is too much air to push around without the benefit of amplification, and on a bad day—solo piano concerts are the worst—the sound just kind of hangs there, and then dissipates, like Lewis Carroll's cat.

Anyway, I was really only suggesting the relative merits of Carnegie Hall, my very favorite place for this sort of hootenanny, but it was too late. Clearly I had shit the bed.

"It does not become you to criticize Lincoln Center," I was told. "Now you think you are smarter than Lincoln Center?"

I probably should have just packed it in right there and headed for the nearest bar. But before I sulked off, I had to mention that I had just been to Lincoln Center that week, where I saw part of a Stravinsky cycle. I wrote a review of it and wanted to send it to him. Maybe seeing my name over a newspaper column might impress him.

"Stravinsky is dissonant. I don't like it," he told me. "I don't know anyone who does."

Really, Dad? *No one?*

I suggested that there was a lot more to Stravinksy than "Rite of Spring," which I correctly assumed he was talking about, because that is all any casual fan ever knows. I suggested that Beethoven, for instance, also used some pretty nifty dissonances and cacophony, especially in his Fifth and Ninth Symphonies, but also in the Third and the Seventh, some of the better piano sonatas, and the Late Quartets. But we were not going to be discussing Beethoven, or much else for that matter.

"Beethoven isn't dissonant," he told me. "You don't know what you are talking about."

There is a wonderful book, *The Lexicon of Musical Invective*, by the composer and conductor Nicolas Slonimsky, which collects contemporaneous reviews of famous composers, from Beethoven to Wagner. All of the reviews are bad. You can look up key phrases in the *Lexicon*—critical jewels like "incoherent mass of rubbish," which will lead you to Wagner; "drooling and emasculated," which takes you to Mahler; and "incomprehensible union of strange harmonies," "obstreperous meowing," and "wrong notes," all of which bring you to

Beethoven, because there is more clanging in those big symphonies than in a prison riot. It is no wonder they were considered monstrosities by the sonically unadventurous when they first hit air.

Anyway, "obstreperous meowing" aside, what my dad was trying to articulate, of course, was that *his* Beethoven was better than *my* Beethoven.

I realized that the old man had no idea what he was listening to and that he didn't really care, which made sense—in my whole life, I had never once heard him play music at home. My parents owned exactly two long-playing phonograph records, the soundtrack to *Man of La Mancha*, and something by the Ink Spots, and they never played either of them. In the car he played the "beautiful music" station—not "light classical," or "adult soft rock," or even "easy listening," but Muzak®—the genuine article—and it made me nuts riding anywhere with him when I was a kid. Who would want to listen to elevator music by choice? And wasn't he worried he'd fall asleep and wreck the car and kill everyone in it?

But I tried very hard to share the music I liked with him, looking for some common ground we could cohabitate on and feel smart together. I remember when I was thirteen and got my first cassette deck, I painstakingly prepared tapes for us to listen to in the car together on long rides, featuring some of the Beatles more effete offerings—"Michelle," "Penny Lane," "Yesterday," etc. I didn't even like these songs (when it comes to the Beatles, I've always been more of a "Helter Skelter" kind of guy), but I figured it was pretty close to the dentist-office crap he was into (they even played versions of all of those songs on the "beautiful music station"). Perhaps, if I could get him to cop to liking the Beatles, then at least our worlds would touch, ever so tangentially, and maybe he would realize that I wasn't simply a witless wrestling fan. I was even willing to keep my mouth shut during "Rocky Raccoon." No sacrifice was too great if it would have helped our relationship.

Those tapes never made it into the dashboard tape player. "I don't want to hear it," he told me flatly. "Put it away. I don't like your music." This was the party line until he was about seventy, when he blurted at an otherwise typically awkward dinner with him, "Oh, I like your kind of music now. I think Buddy Holly is terrific."

I have no idea where this came from. Maybe he was having dinner at a rich friend's house, where some oldies happened to be playing while they had wine and cheese, and this is what he came away with. I ribbed him that he was only about sixty years behind the curve ("What, were you waiting for the lines to die down?") and that maybe if he lived for another sixty, he'd start digging the Sex Pistols. At least he laughed at that.

"Do you know who the Sex Pistols are?" I had to ask.

"I am assuming they are one of *your* punk rock bands."

"Well, not one of mine, per se, but sure, I'll accept that."

"And how is *your* band doing?"

"Well, we're doing pretty good, actually. Playing a lot, having fun. But it's not like we're the Rolling Stones or nuthin' . . ." And then I asked, because I can never be sure of what he did or didn't know, "Do you know who the Rolling Stones are?"

"Yes," he said. "They are a *successful* rock band."

Every once in a while he won a round.

MY FATHER TRULY WAS HIS MOTHER'S SON. She was also a *habituant* of the concert hall, attending Friday afternoon concerts by the Boston Symphony with her sisters, followed by high tea at the Ritz-Carlton on Arlington Street.

Ironically, during the years that she was attending, the music director, Serge Koussevitzky, was responsible for supporting and commissioning some pretty far-out modernists like Prokofiev, Bartók, and that crazy Stravinsky. Whether she knew it or not, she was getting hit with some pretty hip shit. But for her, going to the symphony had little to do with music. It was just what rich old ladies did.

My dad didn't empathize or sympathize when his kids were sad or sick or happy or in pain or victorious or suffering defeat, so he wasn't suddenly going to be transported by the pathos of Beethoven's Ninth or Mahler's Second, never mind the bathos of Sgt. Slaughter vs. The Iron Sheik.

What he never got, or didn't want to accept, was that digging Beethoven didn't make you a genius any more than liking professional wrestling made you a boob. Nor were they mutually exclusive. Sometimes I even watch wrestling with the sound turned off while listening to the Fifth Symphony, which just proves it. Then again, I also like to watch baseball while listening to Aerosmith, so maybe not . . .

WrestleMania and *Idomeneo* live on the same continuum of drama and entertainment. The Marx Brothers, *Star Wars*, *Glengarry Glen Ross*, *A Chorus Line*, *Jaws*, *M*A*S*H*, *The Twilight Zone*, *Romeo and Juliet*, and *West Side Story* probably fall somewhere in between. But isn't *West Side Story* just another staged battle blown up into a ridiculous, massive spectacle?

Actually, when it comes to *West Side Story*, I'm with Pauline Kael. I find the whole thing a bit bumptious. But what the hell do I know. Anyway, I don't go to the symphony because it makes me feel smart, I go because it makes me feel *whole.*

But, to hear my father tell it, classical music is a mon-eyed avocation—not for me—and he began bragging to me about a fund-raiser he had held at his house for his local well-meaning, but ultimately undistinguished, philharmonic.

"So, basically," I ribbed him, because I never learn, "you are helping to fund an unpopular form of music that is wholly unsustainable without grants and subsidies. Hey, if that's what you're into, I could really use a new guitar." I thought that was pretty funny, but I was wrong.

"You need to grow up," he told me. Nothing had really changed since I brought home fifteen cents' worth of Atomic FireBalls.

Then one night he called me up and told me I should stop playing music altogether.

"Huh?"

"You think you are a big shot, but you are not. No one cares about your music. If you were any good, you would have made it by now."

I honestly had no idea where this was coming from. It was very much out of the blue. The guy never called to see how I was. He forgot my birthday more than once.

"I've been thinking about it, and I think you should stop. No one wants to hear you," he said.

I had no response.

"You once told me how happy playing music makes you," he continued, and I wasn't sure where he was going with this, but I had to agree with that. It was true.

"Absolutely," I said, "I am pretty much happiest when I am playing, no question about it. It brings me a great deal of joy."

"But you can't make a living doing it, so you should quit now. It's a waste of time."

It really was just an awful non-conversation, and I never quite figured out what precipitated it. I hung up the phone fairly distressed. Then I sat down on the couch and picked up my Telecaster®. I strummed the chords to "Boom, Boom." It felt pretty good. I picked up my Les Paul® and played a Chuck Berry riff. It weighed a ton and felt even better. I shrugged and decided to put new strings on both guitars, and then go shopping for a new amplifier.

I understood why he hated it when I started playing the drums—they were a *low* instrument, the Yiddish of the musical hierarchy. And *drummers*, oy! Not fit for polite society. But playing the drums was the one thing that gave me confidence when I got to college, and they were eventually my ticket to adventure. Why did he keep telling me I sucked, when clearly I didn't? No drums, no plane tickets to Tokyo. No flights to Amsterdam, Berlin, London, Madrid, Paris, or Zurich, never mind Austin,

New Orleans, Seattle, Los Angeles, San Francisco, or Las Vegas. Later on, when I started playing the guitar seriously, I was doing monthlong tours of France, playing blues and gospel in bars and clubs for two hundred euros a night.

I think all together I must have played about 1,000 gigs, which may or may not sound like a lot, but to put it in some sort of perspective, in the course of their careers the Ramones played 2,280 shows; the Grateful Dead, 2,318. Led Zeppelin, about 600. I have also played on about a dozen records, some of them pretty good.

IF THERE WERE A THOUSAND GIGS, then there must have been at least two thousand rehearsals. That's a lot of playing nice with others.

My father once asked me if I considered myself "a professional musician." I said sure—I show up on time, sober, dressed for the gig, knowing all the songs, ready to go. That is what is called being "professional." But I know he was looking for a dollar amount. And sometimes we made pretty good dough. Sometimes I came back from a tour with a ton of cash (or I'd just hang around in Paris and spend it before I came home). Other times, not so much.

I've played in circus tents and at universities, in art galleries, butcher shops (paid in pork chops), liquor stores (paid in booze), Wall Street strip clubs, French sportatoriums, a famous Brooklyn haberdashery (paid in hats), anarchist squats in Holland and Germany, street fairs, festivals, house parties, libraries, breweries, war zones, weddings, BBQ joints (paid in meat *and* money), on boardwalks and beaches, and in Eastern European theaters so baroque they bordered on rococo. I did a gig in a pizza parlor in Chicago once, and they named a pizza after me—"the Mike Edison Dirty Pie." That was a good day. But every gig is a privilege. I take nothing for granted. Lots of people far more talented than I am never get out of the garage.

All of this made my father angry. "I hate that you get to live your dreams before I get to live mine," he growled.

My mother didn't exactly discourage me, but she wasn't much better. She was certainly no fan of the modern drum set.

"I wish you would have taken piano lessons," she used to sigh.

"I wanted to, if you remember. I was in sixth grade. I played the piano they had in the band room at school one day, and I really liked it, and I came home all excited and asked if we could get a piano and you told me *no.*"

"Your father wouldn't get one, he thought it was a waste of money. You could have played guitar . . . like the ones at summer camp. What do you call those guitars? That's what I would have wanted for you. You could have played for children. You would have been good at that."

"An *acoustic* guitar? Actually, Mom, I do play the guitar. Acoustic *and* the other kind. I've been playing them for about twenty years. You've seen me play—don't you remember that picnic when I played the guitar and sang a few songs?"

"That was you? I thought you played the drums."

There was no winning with these people.

What I came to realize was that my father, not being creative himself, was simultaneously jealous and distrustful of those who were. Except those who were successful, if their paintings represented an asset that he could hang on his wall, or if he could somehow benefit socially from the association. But mostly artists were agents of chaos. He was threatened by people who didn't prioritize making money. It confused him, and confusion was a dissonance that truly made him angry. Musicians were the worst—they undermined his entire worldview by actually having fun while they weren't making money.

Which goes a long way to explaining why ten-year-old me trying to learn how to play the saxophone struck terror into his heart. Maybe that's why, forty years later, he was still trying to pour water on me. I was a time bomb, ticking.

14

I AM JUST A JEEPSTER FOR YOUR LOVE

Recently I told a friend that I was working on a new book. "Something of a childhood memoir, largely about my relationship with my father. It's called *You Are a Complete Disappointment*—his last words to me."

"Oh shit, really?"

And then he laughed. As I've said before, it's like ringing a bell. I've told the story two dozen times, and without exception the person I am talking to laughs, and then immediately apologizes for laughing. "Oh, man, that is horrible, I am so sorry that happened to you."

And then they laugh some more, because it *is* funny, at least if you look at it straight-on: An old man calls his son over to his deathbed, and then just when it seems like it is going to be one of those touching father-son scenes we always imagine, Dad smashes the kid over the head with the emotional equivalent of a folding chair. It would have played well in any number of comedies. Woody Allen could have dined out on that for years.

Recently, one of my friends added to the equation. "That sucks," he said. "I was right there when my dad died. He told me he was proud of me, and then turned to my mom and said 'I hate you, and have always regretted marrying you. You were the biggest mistake of my life.' And then he closed his eyes and that was it. That kinda fucked *her* up for a while."

"Yeah, I'll bet," I laughed, and then I apologized for laughing, before starting up again, because it *was* funny. How could she not see that coming?

UNTIL I BEGAN WRITING THIS, I didn't for a second think that beyond the obvious there was anything my father and I had in common. But it's interesting what you find out when you start asking questions. Maybe it's no surprise that a man so obsessed with being perfect—a father who couldn't suffer less-than-stellar saxophone playing from a ten-year-old, or tolerate earnest idealism in a teenager—was hiding some sort of rhubarb in his own closet. There had to be *some* inadequacy that was chewing at him.

Despite what I had been led to believe, my father never graduated from the MIT business school. I was always told he went to Brown, and then MIT for a master's in business. The fact that he never finished had been willfully overlooked. I never would have known if not for an offhand comment my mom made to me when I had asked her to confirm the year he graduated from MIT, mainly just to keep my time line straight.

"Nineteen sixty-two. His mother wouldn't let him get married until he graduated, that's why we were supposed to wait. But now that I think about it, I don't think he ever finished. He was in a real hurry to get married."

Being a journalist has its advantages. All it took was for me to put my press card in my hatband and politely ask around the MIT registrar's office to confirm that his obligations to graduate were never met, and that no degree was ever conferred. In other words, he dropped out . . . for a chick!

And that chick was my mother!

It was almost too crazy to fathom. My old man, the rebel!

Actually, I had heard a story from one of his cousins that he had wanted to get married while he was still in high school. He had a girlfriend of some sort, and told his mom that he was going to marry her, and she (his mother, that is) said "absolutely not"—he was only sixteen years old, and that is *certainly* not how it was done in *Boston*—and he was just crushed. I guess he was pretty desperate for affection, an affliction to which I can relate, which sucks, because when I see myself in him I end up despising us both, which I admit is pretty twisted.

I remember being so devastated when I broke up with my first girlfriend that I was actually writing *poetry*. And yet somehow I got over it—I found another girlfriend and started writing prose. I was never so freaked out about the *future* that I would ever let it be the enemy of the *now*. But in Dad's worldview, getting hitched must have seemed like the one irrevocable solution to filling that void permanently—so much so that he dropped out of school in the final lap to throw himself at marriage like some lovelorn Quixote. Sadly, it was only thirteen years (and three kids) later when he decided that he had backed the wrong pony and was acting out in pizza restaurants.

MAYBE FIBBING ON YOUR RÉSUMÉ isn't the worst crime? There is no denying my father was gifted at business. In fact, put at the top of *my* list of disappointments that I didn't inherit the gene that makes one excel at earning money. Mostly I just got the genetic code for male-pattern baldness.

Short of actually getting a diploma to hang on the wall, whatever they taught him in school worked like a charm, but that little omission was downright *oily* coming from a guy who browbeat me terribly that "not finishing something you started" was the distinct hallmark of "lack of character," and not the sign of someone likely to "ever be successful." He had used this reasoning to spin my college career as some sort of cautionary tale for my younger brothers.

Coming home from the hospital with Brother No. 1, the night when the old man shot his last breath telling me what a colossal bummer I had been, emotions were running pretty high, as you can imagine. We drove in silence for a few minutes, tooling through the hospital exit and out onto the freeway before he got into it with me.

"Dad was right. If you didn't drop out of school, your life would be a lot better right now."

"Hey, get off my case, toilet face. No, seriously . . . It was thirty freaking years ago. I'm doing just fine."

"You'd be a lot more successful now if you had finished college. That's just how the game is played."

"I'm not playing the same game you are, or haven't you noticed? And the only thing you learned in college is how much beer is in a pint. I remember you took a bowling class for credit. By the way, how much beer is in a pint?"

"I don't know. Twenty ounces?"

"I swear I have no idea how you even get through the day."

"It doesn't matter. I have a degree, you don't. Which makes me smarter than you. I'll show you my last year's tax return, which proves it."

"Did I write the essay on your grad school application?"

"You helped."

"So where's my cut? I want a piece of this action."

"Very funny. Dad gave you two bites at the apple, and you failed both times. My kids are going to college. And if they drop out, I'll cut them off, too, just like Dad did to you. You deserved it."

That wasn't my brother talking; that was the old man talking *through* him. "You had two bites at the apple"— that was word-for-word from the old man's playbook. I had heard it many times before, although I still had no idea what it meant. He had a quiverful of this folksy crap. "You should stop fishing and start cutting bait" was his favorite.

The old man had done a pretty good job of painting me as some sort of a black sheep to my younger brothers. Then again, I didn't really need his help. I did a good job of painting myself a very decent shade of indigo without anyone's malevolent charity.

"Remember the time you vomited out your bedroom window? That was classic."

It was pretty good. I drank the better half of a bottle of Canadian whiskey I found in the basement, left over from their bar mitzvah (marginally less crappy than mine was), and then puked out my second-floor bedroom window, since I knew I would never make it to the bathroom. The entire front of the house was covered in vomit, and the next day both my parents, in a rare joint appearance, monitored me from the front lawn like a couple of UN peacekeepers as I washed off the house with a garden hose. A few neighbors observed from a safe distance. I was sixteen, about par for the course. I didn't regain my sense of humor for *hours*.

"What about the time you came home at six a.m. from a Grateful Dead concert and Mom tried to make you go to school?"

"What about the time . . . What about the time . . . Blah blah blah . . ."

"What about the time YOU GUYS NEVER GOT IN ANY TROUBLE AT ALL???" That usually shuts them up.

Both of my brothers, it seemed, were fairly certain that I had made a hash out of my life, which they saw reductively enough as a series of bad choices. At dinner not too long after Dad died and the Summer of Suck had begun taking casualties, they demanded to know just *how did I measure success?* Because being forty-plus years old, single, unemployed, and in mourning for a cat was clear proof that I was not even remotely in possession of the formula. I am sure my father would have had some earthy bromide to illustrate the point.

"Well," I offered, "I can't afford a Kandinksy for my beach house, but that's okay, because I can't afford a beach house, either."

That might have been a bit *zen* for them. Also, I am not sure that they knew what a "Kandinksy" was. For all I know, they thought it was a kind of sandwich, which would understandably have confused them. I tried again.

"Well," I said, "how about, how much time you spend smiling?"

They pondered that for a few hot moments, but they were still looking for something more, well, *quantifiable*.

Numbers are good. They are, as Timothy Leary once said, maybe the best way to describe objective reality, if there actually is such a thing. That's one reason he loved baseball so much, because baseball had come up with an astonishingly accurate way to describe its own universe. Baseball stats bordered on kabbalah—you could look at them and divine the order of things. The numbers didn't lie. If a guy couldn't hit left-handers, and a lefty came in from the bullpen, you'd best start thinking about pinch-hitting for him.

More important, baseball is a sport *measured in failure*. Failing to get a hit 60 percent of the time is considered excellent: It means you are batting .400, and you will be rated as one of the greatest hitters in the history of the sport. For a baseball team, winning one hundred games in a season is a benchmark for success. But in a 162-game season, it also implies *losing* 62 games. That's a lot of drinking beer in the shower wondering what the hell just went wrong. Still, it could be worse. You could lose 120 games, an all-time low, like the New York Mets did their very first season. Then again, they were still getting paid to play baseball.

I ALWAYS THOUGHT that if I had met the right woman, and that having children were the natural extension of our love, I would have been all-in. I think I would have been a terrific dad. At any rate, that's what people keep telling me.

It didn't work out that way—I just didn't meet the right girl at the right time. But in no way does it compromise or diminish the love I have in my heart. I love kids and can generally relate to them pretty well. The eight-year-old with the hyperactive imagination; the disenchanted, hormone-crazed fourteen-year-old; and the insouciant fifteen-year-old pothead are still alive and (more or less) well somewhere inside of me. And that's not to mention the three-year-old who loved to run around the house wearing a blanket as a cape and screaming "Superman!" at the top of his lungs; the eight-year-old who built the computer; and especially the child who grew up suffering for some love and attention from his dad.

I have lots of friends who are parents, and I am always amazed at what great moms and dads they are. I watch them answer their children's every question and speak to them like adults. They don't talk down; they are patient, playful, and interested. What is really amazing— they sometimes find that they actually like the same things, like superhero movies or hip-hop. I guess that's the post-modern world for you.

And, since these are *my* friends we are talking about, you can bet that they have also enjoyed their fair share of teenage hijinks. You would think that they'd be generally unflappable, since they embrace the basic job description of a teenager as being "to get into trouble." At some point you have to figure that if your kid doesn't break curfew at least once, or give you a hard time, then he is just not trying hard enough.

But I have seen the best parents in the world be ter-rorized by children who have misunderstood the "get in trouble" clause in their contracts as "be a complete fuckup." And then what do you do? The cops call in the middle of the night—"Johnny got popped tagging the school with a can of spray paint," or worse, "Johnny's got a gun." It must be seriously fucking scary when your kid goes very wrong.

Before we became of age to actually raise children, whenever the topic came up among my friends, the great-est fear seemed to be that our kids would grow up to be squares. We used to joke about hiding our favorite, most subversive records—*Raw Power*, *Kick Out the Jams*, *Trout Mask Replica*—but not *so* well that our kids wouldn't find them. And when they did, they would think it was contraband, attach a high value to every note and groove, and forge themselves in a crucible of cool.

I have one pal—the only guy I knew in junior high school with whom I am still friends—who has done a great job of teaching his kids to question authority, as we did when we were kids. They will accept no bullshit. They ask direct questions. If you get caught patronizing them or condescending to them, they will cut you in half. They are awesome young versions of human beings—and a huge annoyance to their teachers and their friends' parents, who consider their impudence a bad example for their own children, who are starting to ask too many damn questions. My friend is understandably very proud.

My biggest fear these days certainly wouldn't be that my kids would turn out to be—God forbid—the kind of little terrors who track mud through the house, or the dunces who comes in *third* in the spelling bee, or the slobs who never learn the difference between their salad fork and the dinner fork. But what if they have no awe of nature? What if they aren't interested in the world around them? What if they think making money is more important than making love? What if they are jerks? What if they are mean?? And what if they get sad, or depressed, or sick? What if they have *problems*? What if they are *human*? It happens.

What can you do? Well, if your daughter wants to go to the ballet, you take her. If your son wants to play baseball, you play catch with him and teach him that real men throw the breaking ball on full count. And if he wants to go to the ballet, you take him, and encourage him. Tell him Baryshnikov got more pussy than Frank Sinatra. Unless he's not into pussy, in which case—who cares, you love him just the same. Ditto, you play ball with the girl if that's what she wants. Maybe she's going to be the baseball star and get lots of pussy. As long as they are kind, and happy, and healthy, I really don't know what more you can ask for.

AFTER MANLY, MY CHAMPION OF A CAT, DIED, I got a new kitten. He was a very wounded rescue, picked up in Ditmas Park, Brooklyn, by some crazy cat ladies and delivered to me on Christmas Eve. He was a Christmas miracle! In fact, I was going to name him Christmas but one of my female friends told me that a cat named "Christmas" could be a liability for a straight, single dude, and that I might want to rethink that. (I still think it is a sweet name.) Anyway, I finally landed on "Jeepster," after the T. Rex song, which was actually a failed attempt to name him "Jupiter," after the Mozart symphony. I had a few in me at the time, but that's another story. Anyway, the point here is that he was the worst kitten imaginable.

Jeepster was gorgeous—about the size of a tennis ball, all-white fur, with a nose the color of bubble gum and beautiful eyes like Errol Flynn or Elvis Presley—but unlike those guys, he had a thing for peeing in my laundry. And then on my couch. He'd pull towels off the rack and pee on them, too. And then he would hide for days.

He was clearly terrified—a dog had bitten him before he was rescued, and he was just so traumatized. I felt awful for him. But there was a point when I was faced with making a pretty tough decision—the cat was making my house smell and had turned my life into some sort of waking nightmare, never knowing when he was going to be inspired to mark his territory. One of my neighbors complained about the smell. I had a date over one time, and he managed to find her coat hanging in the closet, pulled it down, and let her have a dose of his finest. Needless to say, despite cunning and stealth worthy of a Navy SEAL Black Ops Team, she was not impressed.

I truly didn't know what I was going to do with him. Even my vet told me that I had to consider my own happiness—he wasn't advocating anything per se, but I couldn't let the cat take over my life and make me miserable, either. But, in the end, there was no way I was going to do anything drastic with kitty Jeepster.

Not giving up was the right answer. Every day I picked him up and told him that I loved him. I know—he is just a cat, not a child. I'm not that confused. But like I say, sometimes you just have to take it where you find it. He taught me more about patience and unconditional love than I had ever known.

He peed in my laundry, so I picked him up and told him I loved him. I tried to take him to the vet for a checkup, and he sliced me up like a brisket. I looked like Iggy Pop after a particularly rough night. But I picked him back up and told him I loved him.

And then one day, Jeeps turned the corner and decided to be the best cat ever—loyal and loving and impossibly purry and trusting, perhaps my greatest success story. He was on his way to kitty reform school or worse, and with a little love and encouragement, he blossomed into a rock star.

I grew up in a jungle. Pretty much everyone who was a little kid in the early '70s did. It was like a minefield out there—today's stroller brigade would *plotz* if they saw the environment we grew up in. There was secondhand smoke everywhere—the park, the shopping mall, on airplanes. They used to let you smoke in *hospitals*. Both my parents used to smoke in the car, with the kids in the front seat. Special car seats for kids? Air bags? Forget about it. I didn't even see a seat belt until I was seventeen.

The playgrounds we were dropped off in were populated by metal jungle gyms and slides that broiled in the sun—I don't know a single child who didn't suffer second-degree burns every August from a swing set that had cooked to near incandescence. The sandbox (do they even have those anymore?) hid shards of broken glass and dog poop. No one wore helmets, ever, on bikes or on skateboards or snow sleds, the old Flexible Flyers with the sharp blades. We used to run them at breakneck speed down a hill that faced a highway, and if you couldn't turn in time you had to bail out and watch the sled careen across two lanes of traffic, praying that it would make it without being run over by the next Chevy Impala that came flying by. The alternative—not ditching and dying—was only marginally worse.

There was zero supervision. There was blood everywhere. My neighborhood was a cabbage patch of skinned knees and elbows, cracked foreheads, and missing teeth. We played street hockey of such a violent nature that we once assessed a two-minute penalty for crying. Kids got stitched up all the time. When I came home beaten up, I didn't get a second look. It was all very normal back then.

I was a latchkey kid, the product of what they now call "free-range parenting"—some sort of backlash to the insanely paranoid helicopter parents who fret about every moment of little Jack and Jill's over-structured life and every morsel of organic mush that goes into their mouths. Today's mommies and daddies would be appalled at the crap I was fed as a kid. Health food was for weirdos. Never mind the prefab and frozen dinners, my mother thought Marshmallow Fluff® was a vegetable. She fed me Twinkies® and Drake's® cakes every day for lunch. Breakfast was nonexistent, unless she forgot to go shopping for dinner, and then out came the pancake mix. And despite it all, here I am.

Do kids still make spaceships out of washing machine boxes? I used to love that. And when we got tired of playing spaceship, we flipped the box on its side and turned it into a submarine, or a time machine. A high premium was placed on imagination. For better or worse, I never outgrew it.

15

FREEDOM

Listen," Dr. Headshrinker suggested one afternoon, "it's not my job to tell you not to come here, but you seem to be doing great. You're doing everything right. You came through it—you may have once been a victim, but you no longer define yourself that way."

"I'm good. I'm actually really happy. I love what I do. I count my blessings every day."

When I lost my job, *time*, as ever, turned out to be the greatest gift of all. After a few months chasing my tail and trying to exorcise the Voice of Disappointment from my head, I scored a cherry gig ghost-writing something of a celebrity chef memoir, which eventually wound up on the *New York Times* Best Seller list, and that came with some nice perquisites attached—four weeks in Italy, vineyard-hopping, being the obvious bell-ringer.

That led to collaborating on another food book, which came with another spectacular passel of perks, including a week on the West Coast, hanging out and performing in San Francisco, Napa Valley, and Portland. Every time I turned around, someone wanted to give me a humanely raised, sustainably farmed steak or a bottle of biodynamic wine. When I got back to New York, I'd get called to do speaking gigs at hipster food events, and I'd bring my guitar and theremin and turn it into a hootenanny.

One night, we had a gig at one of those gorgeous country inns where George Washington allegedly slept, out in Pennsylvania near the Delaware Water Gap. We did a presentation about sustainable farming and heritage breeds for an organic sheepherders association, and they gave me a lamb—an entire, all-natural, hippie lamb. It came shipped, cut into parts, and I spent the next months making dinner for friends. I cooked up a rack of ribs on a cold, rainy night, and grilled chops on the BBQ when summer came. I made chili out of the shoulders and some beautiful *ragù* for pasta. But the best part is that I had the legs cured and turned into prosciutto—lamb prosciutto! It's not for everyone, but if you love lamb, I swear it would make you roll over and purr like a kitten. I would probably have written that book just for the lamb, but the truth is, I got paid enough to keep the lights on for a while *and* I got to share all of this great food with my friends. What more could a fellow ask for?

But there were still plenty of times when I could still hear my father riding me—*You are a complete disappointment! Forty years of nothing!*—namely, every time I got a rejection, which is a big part of being a writer. And a human being, I reckon.

"This isn't about forgiving *and* forgetting. You are still processing," Dr. Headshrinker told me. "What he did to you when he died was pretty rough, but you became the person you wanted to be, not the person you were told to be. You are always going to remember your bad experience with him, and that's a good thing. You need to share it. There are a lot of men who have had fathers who were bullies who need to hear this story. But you can also let go. You forgave the bully in junior high school, after all."

"That wasn't easy. Until I wrote it down, I couldn't even talk about it. I clenched my jaw every time I thought about that kid. But I realized he didn't have it too good at home, either. He was raised to be an animal. It probably doesn't help when your playroom looks like a prison yard."

"Your father had a chance to make peace. What would have happened if he called you over to his hospital bed and said, *I want you to know I am proud of you*? Would that have changed anything that had happened between you up until then?"

"Well, of course not. You can only move forward in time—that is one of the few things I am sure of. But anyway, that is not what happened . . . He couldn't help himself, he doubled down and came after me one more time. He had to have the last word and be the winner."

"Are you still in competition with him?"

"I never was! That's the point. The only person I am in competition with is myself. I can always be a better version of me. Anyway, I'm working on it . . ."

"But if he had said something much different when he died, if he had said that he loved you and that he was proud of you, would you have forgiven him then?"

"I have to think about that. I suppose so . . . I eventually forgave my mother for being such a horror."

"Yes, but you said she apologized."

"Not to me, not exactly, not in so many words. But for a hot second there, she became a bit more self-aware and was more or less contrite for everything. It was the best she was going to be able to do. It couldn't have been easy for her. She made it miserable growing up, but sure, I forgive her. She was in an awful place and didn't handle it very well. She still blamed my father for her misery, and of course she says I didn't make it easy on her, which may or may not be true. She had a victim mentality. But she was out of her depth back then."

"So it's easier to forgive someone who acknowledges their mistakes?"

"Of course. But more important, finally, she gave me the greatest gift of all—she let *me* make *her* happy. In her last moments she allowed me to bring her this great joy. It's a shame it had to wait until she was dying, but that was a very open, pure act of love."

We took a beat to consider that. It had been a real blessing.

"I wonder if your father was ever bullied," she pondered.

"I guess there is no way to tell."

"You could have asked the psychic."

She's a good ribber, Dr. Headshrinker.

"I was thinking about it," I said. "He used to champion an old British television mini series, *Tom Brown's Schooldays*, which was about this perfect, defenseless little babyface kid, away from home for the first time, being hazed and bullied terribly at some posh boarding school. He made me watch it every time it was on. The thing was, it was incredibly sadistic—the most memorable scene was of the bully and his gang of rich assholes literally roasting Tom in front of a fire until he passes out. It was the single cruelest thing I had ever seen as a child—I mean it was just humorless and awful—and we watched it over and over again. Tom would get brutally whipped by the schoolmaster for things he didn't do. He was caned, mercilessly. They had a special tower for it. He was always set up by the bully, who seemed to get away with everything. It was this gleefully drawn-out sadism that my father loved. I guess the bully finally gets his comeuppance in the end, but by that point, who really cares? All that sticks in my mind is Tom getting beaten up and burned. I guess it's worth mentioning that the bully was very charismatic. His name was Flashman, and I remember he wore this terrific top hat. Anyway, here's the thing—after all of this thinking and writing and reflection, I still don't know if my dad related to Flashman or to Tom. That's kind of fucked up."

I HAD BEEN READING ABOUT the concept of Jewish forgiveness, and let me tell you, we are some tough customers. We're not in the business of giving away anything for free. There is always a big NO to easy forgiveness. On the other hand, if there is some overwhelming need for forgiveness—and we could be talking about a crippling debt, for instance—then you *have* to give it. And if you offer it, it is only *mensch*-like to accept it. But the forgiven need to show some repentance, too. That's part of the social contract.

There is more: If you have been abused, there is absolutely no moral obligation to forgive the abuser, but you also have the option for some sort of in-between deal where you may offer some half-assed pardon and forgive the debt, but not the crime. The greatest act of forgiveness is to achieve a pure type of empathy, to embrace the person who has hurt you and take them into your heart. You have achieved understanding, without equivocating, that people are frail, that humans are flawed, that we all deserve love and sympathy—which I agree with 100 percent. Except, of course, some people are just dicks and don't make it all that easy.

Christians, on the other hand, are pushovers. They give away forgiveness like wax teeth on Halloween. Jesus was obviously very big on it, but I think He understood, too, that turning the other cheek was counterintuitive—it just isn't the first reaction most people have after being slugged, and it kind of makes you an easy mark for the next time. But hey—judge not lest ye be judged, forgive and ye shall be forgiven, and all that. It's not the worst thing anyone has ever said.

Jews want to break everything down and negotiate like a bunch of fucking lawyers. Also, while we excel at asking questions, we can be pretty squirrelly when it comes to providing answers. Christians cut right through any Socratic shilly-shallying with pure faith—you have to believe and you have to forgive, because that's what God wants. Jesus says it's the only way to roll. I guess they don't remember that whole vengeful-God thing: The Old Testament is just teeming with floods and fires and smiting, always lots of smiting.

Neither approach was really my style. I was never going to completely parse the molecularly complex Talmudic teachings and anecdotes that make up Jewish tradition—the most eggheaded rabbis in the business are still trying to make horse sense of that mess—nor was I suddenly to become so Christ-like that I stopped punching back. Anyway, if it doesn't really come from inside of you, then what is it really worth?

And then I read this Buddhist parable: There are two monks who find each other on the road, years after they had been in prison together, where they had been brutally tortured. I have no idea who would have tortured a couple of Buddhists, or why it seems like monks are always running into each other on some road—apparently that's just what they do. Anyway, one monk says to the other, "Have you forgiven them?" Meaning the people who had tortured them. And the other says, "Never! I will never forgive them!" And the first monk says, "Well, then I guess you're still in prison. Call me when you get out."

Instead of holding a grudge, I finally came around and just said, "What's the fucking point?" After everything, it was that simple.

Well, let's be honest, it took a while to get there. Hours on Dr. Headshrinker's couch. I had to write an entire freaking book. But I had fun doing it. That's not exactly how the Jews or Christians teach forgiveness, but as I keep saying, sometimes you just have to take it where you find it—rescued cats, Buddhists, *Jackass*, Beethoven, whatever.

I want to be happy, and so I am. It takes some work, but there you have it. My parents were miserable because that's the choice they made. They didn't make happiness a priority. My brothers, and my dad's wife, especially, would argue that I am wrong—look how *happy* and *successful* your father was! But if you find yourself on your deathbed using your very last breath to rip into your kid because of his taste for professional wrestling, I think it is fair to say you have some seriously unresolved issues.

Speaking of wrestling, there is an old tradition that when a wrestler retires, he goes "out on his back." That means putting the next guy *over*. It's the honorable thing to do. When you leave, you use your legacy to make someone else look good. You shine a little light. Maybe it's just good business, to keep the show on the road, but it seems like pretty good karma to me, too. I think you should always leave things a little bit better than when you found them. Somehow even my mom managed to pull that rabbit out of her hat.

It still breaks my heart—my dad dying with so much anger in him. I think about it every day. There is a lot I haven't even told you—just awful conversations, rotten, despicable hoodoo, a lifetime's worth of put-downs. There was no playfulness and no shared joy. No *naches*. Did being mean to me make him feel better about himself? I can't imagine that it did. What did any of it prove? It was all so needless.

I remember when I got the call that he had died, the day after I left him in the hospital. I wept, just as any father's son would, and then I cried some more because I was thinking about the last thing that he said to me, screaming at me through an oxygen mask that I was such a disappointment. No matter how funny it may seem from a safe distance—the setup, the delivery, the flawless timing—at that moment you can be very sure I wasn't laughing. I just wish he knew how much I loved him.

I can't help but feel so terribly sorry for him. He grew up made to feel as if he had to be perfect, terrified of what other people thought. No matter how successful he became otherwise, he never really escaped, and a real meanness snuck in. He did his best to keep me tethered to his fears, but somehow I went wrong—I was able to cut loose and set myself free.

Two feet to the right of where I'm sitting is an old piano—eventually I got around to learning how to play. The piano's been beaten up pretty bad, certainly worse than I ever was. It's a rescue, just like Jeepster the Cat, and who knows just what kind of blues will come out when I put my hands on it? Who knows how many wonderful songs remain unwritten?

Meanwhile, just as soon as I finish writing this, I'm going to drink a beer in the shower and sing along with the cassette of Beethoven's Fifth Symphony (Kleiber conducting the Vienna Philharmonic, natch), which lives in the old boom box I keep in the bathroom. I made the words up myself—they are very dirty and change all the time.

And then, since it's Monday night, I'll be watching wrestling on TV. The new girlfriend can't stand it ("Why do you watch that crap?"), so she'll go to dinner with a friend, and I'll send out for the tandoori platter from Curry in a Hurry and open a ridiculously delicious bottle of Barbaresco—one of two I was given as sort of an honorarium for playing my guitar at a wine tasting a few weeks ago. It's the kind of wine where the cherries and tar leap out of the glass and smack you right on the nose, like a cartoon monkey. It's much better juice than I can usually afford, and if I'm smart, I'll save some to share with the girl, because she practically lives for cartoon monkeys, and if she comes home and there's no wine left, she'll just insist that we open the other bottle. And you know how that goes.

One good thing just leads to another.

ACKNOWLEDGMENTS

Thanks to my incredibly patient editor Melanie Madden, and the entire team at Sterling Publishing. As ever, thanks and undying appreciation to the unflappable Jim McCarthy, Jane Dystel, Miriam Goderich, and everyone at Dystel & Goderich Literary Management. Thanks to Deb Shapiro Publicity, the Heritage Radio Network, and Heritage Foods USA.

For their continued kindness, encouragement, and support, love and huzzahs to Leslie Fabian, Jon Spencer and Cristina Martinez, Judy McGuire, and Lisa Carver.

Extra warm thanks to Eric Winnicki for his numerous contributions, glad you are back.

Thanks to Cynthia Santiglia, Carly Sommerstein, and Todd Hanson for their sage editorial advice.

Thanks to Mickey Finn, "Beatnik No. 1" Bob Bert, and all current and future members of the Space Liberation

Army, the Insterstellar Rendezvous Band, and the Edison Rocket Train.

Very special thanks and all my love to Jeepster the Cat, and Christine "Daisy" Martin, who sleeps at night better than anyone I know.

ABOUT THE AUTHOR

Mike Edison is the former editor and publisher of *High Times* magazine. His books include the celebrated memoir *I Have Fun Everywhere I Go*, the sprawling social history of sex on the newsstand, *Dirty! Dirty! Dirty!* and the deliciously filthy political satire *Bye, Bye, Miss American Pie.* More recently he collaborated with Joe Bastianich on his *New York Times* bestselling memoir, *Restaurant Man*, of which writer Bret Easton Ellis has said, "The directness and energy have a cinematic rush . . . not a single boring sentence." Edison has worked as a foreign correspondent for *Hustler* and was a high-paid gun-for-hire of the legendary *Penthouse* letters. He has contributed to numerous magazines and websites, including *Huffington Post*, the *Daily Beast*, the *New York Observer*, *Spin*, *Interview*, and *New York Press*, for which he covered classical music and professional wrestling. Edison is also an internationally known musician and ferociously dedicated storyteller, and he can be heard every Sunday on his show *Arts & Seizures* on the Heritage Radio Network. He lives and works in Brooklyn.

www.mikeedison.com

You Are a Complete Disappointment
Book interior designed by Janet M. Evans.
Composed in Warnock Pro, which was
created by Adobe staff designer
Robert Slimbach to honor
the co-founder of Adobe
John Warnock.